FROM MOUNTAIN TOPS
TO VALLEY FLOORS

From Mountain Tops to Valley Floors

New Walks with Historic Interest in Gwynedd

Dave Salter & Dave Worrall

ISBN: 0-86381-430-1

Cover: Alan Jones
Photo: Bob Lewis

First published in 1997 by Gwasg Carreg Gwalch,
Iard yr Orsaf, Llanrwst, Dyffryn Conwy, Wales.
☎ 01492 642031

Printed and published in Wales

TO CAROLINE, JO AND SUSIE
WHO LET US HAVE
THE LATE PASSES

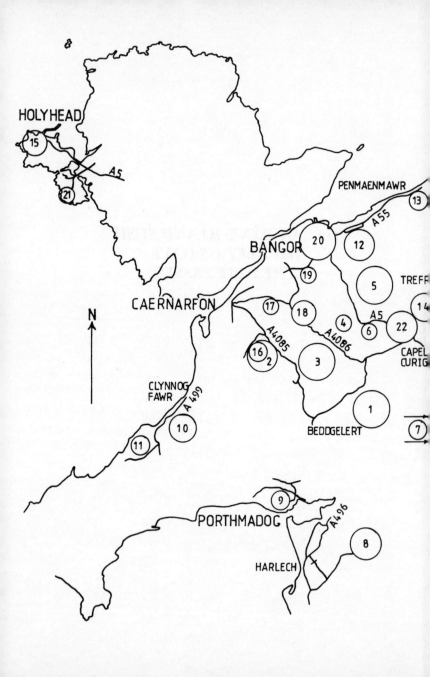

CONTENTS

Walks on the High Tops

Walks on the Lesser Tops

Walks on the Hillsides and Valley Floors

PREFACE

It is undoubtedly true that the more you think you know an area, the more you discover how little you know. We discovered how little we knew a few years ago when we started straying from the more frequented paths. The early revelations were due to the guide books written by Don Hinson. His marvellous books took us into pockets of North Wales that we swore we knew but which we soon discovered we didn't. Clearly as seasoned walkers this was a shock!

Before long the maps were out and long hours spent considering the possibilities. The inspiration for the walks was a desire to fill in the gaps and to explore those areas of which we knew little. Subsequently, although there is no logical sequence to the walks, it is hoped that each excursion will have an attraction. This may be a different perspective on a familiar scene, or an insight into historical events. These walks have given us pleasure and a renewed interest in the marvellous walking to be had in North Wales and along the way a few interesting stories have added spice to steps we have taken. We hope you enjoy following the same steps, whatever the motivation may be.

THE WALKS

Before we tighten up the laces of our walking boots and set off on the walks, it is important to consider some aspects of safety and equipment. There are various books available that cover such aspects in far greater detail and any time spent studying these would be time well spent. We would urge all readers to learn the basic skills of map reading, elements of weather forecasting and fundamental mountaineering skills before they venture forth on any of the walks listed. Even those walks that keep to the lower levels cannot be underestimated. Indeed the walk "Port Penrhyn , Its Railways and Rivers" was once completed in sub zero temperatures and howling gales whilst "Cwm Bychan's Eastern Skyline etc" was enjoyed in the highest temperatures we have experienced on our walks. There is available a forecast for the Snowdonia area on 0891 505330. Indeed in future the weather station on the summit of Snowdon may provide information to the public via an information screen in the Llanberis Museum.

In our experience the most valuable piece of equipment you can take is a good dollop of common sense. If used well it will tell you

when to turn round if the weather turns nasty,
when it's too late in the day to start the walk
you intended and a whole host of other useful
items. Along with this, sturdy walking boots
and adequate warm clothing for the prevailing
conditions plus effective waterproof clothing
make a good start. Add to this the means to
carry the equipment and make sure you put in a
map of the area, a compass and some food for
the day. No doubt there are items that you
would also consider essential, pack them by all
means. The contents of peoples rucsacs is very
much down to an individuals interest. Above all
be safe and remember that the equipment we
take with us is intended to make the day more
enjoyable.

Finally, we would like to thank all those who
have offered advice and helped with
information. Their help has been invaluable.
In many ways their contribution is made
without the reward of completing the walks, but
here we must admit to a selfishness. We have
often completed our walks without meeting
another human being and this has been one of
the attractions. Now we must accept that this
may no longer be the case. Let us do what we
can to ensure that the countryside suffers no

further damage and that we preserve it as best as possible for future generations.

Dave Salter and Dave Worrall.

A GLOSSARY OF PLACE NAMES
FOUND IN THE TEXT

This glossary has been included to enable the walker to appreciate the romantic and diverse nature of the Welsh language. It is an ancient language and steeped in mythology. As with all languages, many of the words when translated into English can have different meanings. It therefore becomes difficult, with place names, to obtain an accurate or logical translation. Those given are those we believe to be relevant.

Abergwyngregyn	Estuary of the white shells
Afon Rhythallt	River of the red wooded hill
Beddgelert	Grave of the dog Gelert or Grave of St Celert (a 6th Century Saint)
Bera Bach	Smaller stack of rocks
Bera Mawr	Larger stack of rocks
Betws-y-coed	Chapel in the trees
Blaen-y-cwm	Front or Head of the valley
Borth-y-gest	Port in the hollow
Braich	Arm
Braich y Dinas	Arm of the fort
Braich Melyn	Yellow arm (of the mountain)
Braich Tu Ddu	Dark side of the spur
Braich Tŷ Du	Spur of the black house
Bryn Bras	Luxuraint hill
Bryn Derwydd	Hill of the Druid
Bron y Foel	Near to the rounded bare mountain
Bronydd Isaf	Lower side of the hill
Bwlch Cywion	Pass of the young sheep
Bwlch y Ddeufaen	Pass of the two stones
Bwlch Ehediad	Pass of the winged fowls
Bwlch Maes Gwm	Pass of the open field
Bwlch Mawr	Large pass
Bwlch y Mignog	Boggy pass

13

Bwlch y Saethau	Pass of the arrows
Bwlch Tyddiad	"Roman steps"
Cader Idris	Chair of the giant Idris
Cae Hir Uchaf	Upper long field
Capel Curig	The chapel of St Curig
Carneddau	Cairns
Carnedd Dafydd	Cairn of Prince Dafydd
Carnedd Llywelyn	Cairn of Prince Llywelyn
Clip	The rise
Clip yr Orsedd	Raise to the throne
Clogwyn	Cliff
Clogwyn Du'r Arddu	The high dark cliff
Cnicht	Knight
Craig	Rock
Craig y Bera	Pyramid like rock
Craig Coch	Red rock
Craig Cwm Bychan	Rock of the small valley
Craig Llwyn	Rock of the copse or grove
Craig Wen	White rock
Craig yr Ysfa	Rock of the craze (when looking over edge)
Creigiau Gleision	Grey-green rocks
Crib	Comb or jagged ridge crest
Crib y Ddysgl	(Jagged) Ridge of the bowl
Crib Lem	Sharp rocks
Cwm	Valley
Cwm Bychan	Small valley
Cwm Caseg	Valley of the mare
Cwm Cywion	Valley of the young sheep
Cwm Ddu	Black valley
Cwm Eigau	Valley of the herds
Cwm Hetiau	Valley of the hats
Cwm Llafar	Valley of the babbling sounds
Cwm y Glo	Valley of charcoal
Cwt y Bugail	Hut of the sheperd
Cytiau	Huts

Cytiau Gwyddelod	Hut of the Irish or foreigner
Dolbadarn castle	Castle on the edge of Llyn Padarn
Drosgl	Stony ground
Elan	Young female deer
Elen (yr)	Mountain of the Princess Helen
Elin	Elbow
Y Faner	'Banner' newspaper
Felin	Mill
Foel	Rounded bare mountain (bald)
Foel Fras	Rough rounded bare mountain
Foel Goch	Red rounded bare mountain
Foel Grach	Scabby rounded bare mountain
Foel Gron	Round, rounded bare mountain
Foel Lus	Bilberry covered round bare mountain
Ffrith Craig	Spotty rock
Gamallt	Crooked hill
Gallt y Celyn	Hill of the holly
Glan Morfa Bach	Edge of the small moor
Glyderau	Dissaray of rocks
Gras	Graceful
Gwern Gof Isaf	Marsh of the upper farm
Gwastad Llyn Coed	Tree of the still lake
Gyrn	Cone
Gyrn Ddu	Black cone
Gryn Goch	Red cone
Hebron	Biblical name from the old non conformist chapel which stood nearby
Helyg	Willows
Llanberis	Church of St Peris
Llech Ddu	Black slate
Lledr	Leather
Lliwedd	In the shade
Llymllwyd	Grey sharp ridge
Llyn	Lake

Llyn yr Adar	Lake of the birds
Llyn Clyd	Sheltered lake
Llyn Colwyd	Beloved lake
Llyn Cwellyn	Lake of the reeds
Llyn y Cŵn	Lake of the dogs
Llyn Edno	Lake of the winged fowls
Llyn Ffynhonnau	Lake of the wells
Llyn Ffynnon y Gwas	Lake of the well of the servant
Llyn Gwynant	Lake of the white stream
Llyn Idwal	Lake of the giant Idwal (Prince)
Llyn Marchlyn Mawr	Large lake of the stallion
Llyn Morwynion	Lake of the maidens
Llyn Pryfed	Lake of the insects
Llyn Twr Glas	Lake of the blue tower
Llynnau'r Cŵn	Lakes of the dogs
Migneint	Boggy plateau
Moel	Rounded bare mountain (bald)
Moel y Ci	Rounded bare mountain of the dog
Moel Cynghorion	Rounded bare mountain of the counsels
Moel y Defaid	Rounded bare mountain of the sheep
Moel Eilio	Woven round bare mountain
Moel y Gest	Rounded bare mountain above the hollow
Moel Lus	Bilberry covered round bare mountain
Moel Meirch	Rounded bare mountain of the maidens
Moel Smytho	Rounded bare mountain of the consoled
Moel Wnion	Rounded bare mountain like an onion
Moel Wian or *Wion*	Rounded bare mountain of Gwion

Moel Tryfan	Rounded bare mountain with three peaks
Moelwyn	White rounded bare mountain
Moelfre	Rounded bare mountain above
Mynydd	Mountain
Mynydd Ddu	Black mountain
Mynydd Twr	Tower mountain (Holyhead mountain)
Nantlle	Lighted water
Nant y Betws	Gorge of the birch grove
Nant Gwrtheyrn	Vortigens ravine
Nefydd Hardd	Nefydd the beautiful (Prince Idwal's assasin)
Pant Hafod Las	Stream of the blue upland dwelling
Pen yr Allt	Top of the hill
Pen yr Helgi Du	Head of the black hunting hound
Pen Llithrig y wrach	Slippery hill of the witch
Penmachno	Head of the river Machno
Penmaenmawr	Head of the big stone
Penrhyn	Headland
Porthmadog	Port designed by William Maddocks
Pont Brwynog	Bridge of the rushes
Rallt Uchaf	Upper hill
Rhaeadr Fawr	Large water falls
Rhinog Fawr	Big threshold
Rhoscolyn	Tail end of the moor
Rhyd Ddu	Black ford
Sarn Helen	Causeway of Princess Elen
Snowdon	Norman word meaning Snow hill
Tal y Fan	End of the peaks
Tal y Waen	End of the marsh
Tomen y mur	Wall of the motte
Tremadog	Town designed by William Maddocks

Trwyn y Gorlech	Nose (headland) of the slope
Tryfan	Three peaks
Twll Du	Black hole (Devil's kitchen)
Tŷ Hyll	Rugged (ugly) house
Tyn Llidiart	Gate house
Tŷ yn y Nos	House in the night (constructed between the hours of sunset and sunrise on common land)
Waen Fawr	Big moor
Wen slab	White slab
Ynysoedd Gwylanod	Seagull islands
Ysbyty Ifan	St. John's hospital
Ysgolion Duon	The Black ladders
Y Clochdy	The Belfry
Y Frith Craig	The Speckled crag
Y Garn	The Cairn
Y Gegin Fach	The Small kitchen
Y Lon Wen	The White road
Y Tylwyth Teg	The fairies
Yr Arig	Long ridge
Yr Eifl	Notch in a fork
Yr Elen	The mountain of Princess Elen
Yr Wyddfa	Snowdon summit, burial place of Rhita Fawr, the giant.

BEDDGELERTS EASTERN PARISH BOUNDARY, ITS LAKES AND WETLAND

Maps 1:50,000 Sheet 115 Caernarfon and Bangor or
1:25,000 Sheet 17 Snowdon and Conwy
Distance 9miles/14.5 kilometres
Height gained 1800ft/548metres
Duration 5.5 Hours
Terrain Good up to highland, very wet in places
thereafter.
Car park In one of the small parking areas close to Llyn
Gwynant G.R.649520

From the Lake side the walk leaves Llyn Gwynant and
climbs up the rhododendron clad flanks of the valley,
passes through pine forests to emerge on to the open
hillside. The path ascends alongside one of the many
tributaries from Llyn Llagi. On the north west shore of the
lake, the remains of an old settlement can be found,
which is thought to be of a *Crannog* or artificial island.
These islands were constructed on and above the water
for security from wild beasts and enemies. These types of
structure were thought to be built by a fair haired race
called the Beaker race. Historians also believe that these
people were known as *Tylwyth Teg* (Fairies) which
subsequent folk tales have corrupted and turned into little
people who live in and around water. After the lake is
passed the path steepens and winds through rocky
outcrops to arrive at the shores of Llyn yr Adar. Here,
views of the Moelwyn range and Cnichts rocky flanks
unfold. They tell a story of the quarrying activities of the
last century and its impact on the landscape. Further in
the distance the tree covered Lledr valley spreads towards
the open moorland of the Migneint. As the ridge line is
traversed spectacular views of the Snowdon massif can be
seen.

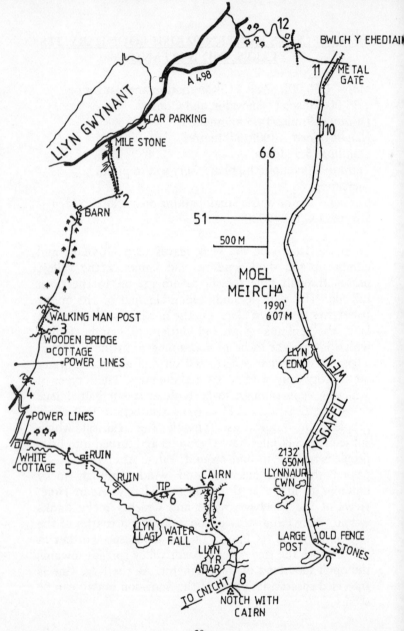

LLYN GWYNANT

A 498

CAR PARKING

MILE STONE
1

2
BARN

WALKING MAN POST
3
WOODEN BRIDGE
COTTAGE
POWER LINES

4

POWER LINES

WHITE
COTTAGE 5

RUIN

RUIN

TIP
6

CAIRN

7

LYN
LLAGI

WATER
FALL

LLYN
YR
ADAR

8

TO CNICHT

NOTCH WITH
CAIRN

12

11

METAL
GATE

10

66

51

500 M

MOEL
MEIRCH
1990'
607 M

LLYN
EDNO

WEN

YSGAFELL

2132'
650 M
LLYNNAUR
CWN

LARGE
POST

OLD FENCE
STONES

9

BWLCH Y EHEDIAD

The ridge line now follows the Parish boundary passing numerous lakes, which many years ago were stocked for the sporting gentry. This gave rise to the abundance of wildlife as the names of the many physical features imply. Llyn yr Adar, Llyn Edno, Llynnau'r Cŵn and Bwlch Ehediad.

In the boggy tract of land close to Bwlch Ehediad lies the remains of an Air Lingus Dakota DC3 "Saint Kevin". In early January 1952 the plane was on a night flight from Northholt to Dublin. The pilot believing he was over the Welsh coast descended from 4500ft and was caught in the severe down draughting of the Snowdonia area and was forced to crash land into the bog. All 20 passengers and the 3 crew perished, not all the bodies being recovered. A memorial plaque on a near by bluff of rock marks the accident site.

The parish boundary passes over the summit of Ysgafell Wen and skirts around Moel Meirch following a new boundary fence, this replaces the much earlier fence which will be seen as rusty old iron fence posts. After extolling the virtues of this excursion it must be pointed out that in its later sections the walk can be very wet and the walker must be under no illusion that he or she will have dry feet at the end. Compensation for this must be the views encountered.

The walk From the car park walk down the road in the direction of Beddgelert. **1.** After passing a milestone L up walled track. Up steps with wall and bushes on L. Do not join track at bend but continue up field with wall and bushes on L. Continue up track with wall on L then with wall on R then soon walled on both sides. **2.** At termination of wall on R (track turns sharp L at this point) into field on R and along grassy track towards barn. L in front of barn through large gate posts L keeping wall on L (with bushes). Over stile and into wood. Over stile and into clearing over stream. Past walking man post and through steel gate. **3.** Over timber bridge and up hillock. Down field towards and under power lines. Cross bridge and continue along rough track. **4.** Over stile to road and L through gate and down track. At L/H bend continue on, along rougher track with fence on R. At white house L up path, under power lines (do not pass house). Up to wall gap and up rough steps. Path now climbs parallel with L/H bank of stream, faint in places. **5.** On reaching low wall path crosses stream. Pass ruin and over stile, path now reverts to L bank. At raise head for wall gap with ruin, path now faint heading into cwm. Head towards main waterfall and on sighting lake on R head L towards walled sheep pen. Through wall gap and up to slate tip, R up path. **6.** Through wall gap. **7.** At large cairn R up faint path , small cairns mark path. At ridge crest small descent then ascend up boulder filled valley. Head for L/H edge of lake and continue round passing over 4 streams into lake. After 4th stream head 1/2 L towards notch in the sky line of ridge. **8.** At cairn in notch L and follow ridge crest uphill on vague path. **9.** At small lake 1/2 L to join path with line of short posts L. At large post R to follow lines of old fence posts. A new fence continues with fence on R. **10.** Two stiles will be noticed, close to each other these can be used to avoid a wet patch. Path drops to large saddle with old wall on R. **11.** Follow wall to metal gate and stile (Bwlch Ehediad) then L down vague path with some cairns to wall. Through narrow wall gap then R keeping wall on R. Cross two low walls and down to ruin. L down path before ruin. **12.** Path drops into wood, continue down to road. Over stile and cross road to next stile. Down steep field to gate and road. L along road and at junction 1/2 R down road to parking area.

Refreshments Dependant on homeward direction, the choice could be The Antiques Shop in Beddgelert, The Pinnacle Cafe in Capel Curig or Pete's Eats in Llanberis.

MYNYDD MAWR

Maps 1:50,000 Sheet 115 Caernarfon and Bangor or
1:25,000 Snowdon and Conwy sheet 17
Distance 6.5 Miles/10 Kilometres
Height gained 2320ft/707 Metres
Duration 5 Hours
Terrain High mountain terrain with rough ground and
later some boggy patches
Car park At G.R.523585 on the side of the road .

Astute readers will notice that this walk shares much of
its route with the Kate Roberts walk. However, the
nature of the two walks are quite different. The Kate
Roberts walk is a relatively low level route which would be
well suited to a family looking for some adventure, whilst
the top of Mynydd Mawr is a true mountain top. Its
location is quite remote and its paths are seldom walked.
Those looking to avoid the crowds of walkers on the other
peaks in the area may find this route suited to their
needs.

In the not too distant future however, the valley of Nant y
Betws will echo to the sound of steam trains. The Welsh
Highland railway is being resurrected and the first section
from Caernarfon to Llanwnda should start to be
constructed in 1997. The original route was from
Caernarfon to Porthmadog, and eventually the plan is to
recreate the whole route. This may well bring the
possibility of some fine walks using the train as a link.

The mountain Mynydd Mawr has long been known
locally as Elephant mountain due to its resemblance to a
reclining elephant. This is perhaps best observed from
the Caernarfon direction. As the flanks are climbed views

24

expand over Anglesey, across to Moel Eilio and the South Nantlle ridge. Later the towers and gullies in Cwm Du provide spectacular scenery, as does Craig y Bera on the descent from the summit. For such a well rounded mountain, the steepness of some sides is a revelation. This fact was however known to the Romans. Tradition has it that Mynydd Mawr was used by the Romans for the execution of criminals. They were taken to the cliffs of Craig y Bera and placed into wooden cages which were then hurled over the edge. Presumably few survived the subsequent plunge.

The dwellings known as Tŷ yn y Nos were also common in the area. As in the story of the Ugly House near Betws-y-Coed, these houses were constructed in a single night between the dusk and dawn. This feat being achieved, the builder of the house was allowed to claim the land that was contained within an area marked by throwing an axe from each corner of the house. These houses were built on common land, but local landowners such as Lord Newborough tried to stop this practice with the introduction of the Enclosure Act in 1827. Fortunately this failed and the practice continued for a short while, much to the delight of the local population.

The walk L out of car park. After 25 metres 1/2 R along track to follow wall on L. **1.** After gate to Penrallt take R/H fork in track. Along with wall kept on R. **2.** From wall corner, follow meandering track to top of hill. Head down to wall corner near Forest boundary. Follow wall on L. **3.** Past kissing gate on L and follow path straight on and over stream. **4.** At wall corner, with enclosed gate go L keeping wall on L. After 75 metres go R to cross small stream to pick up faint path running 1/2 R across hillside to small cairn. Faint path ascends a broad shoulder

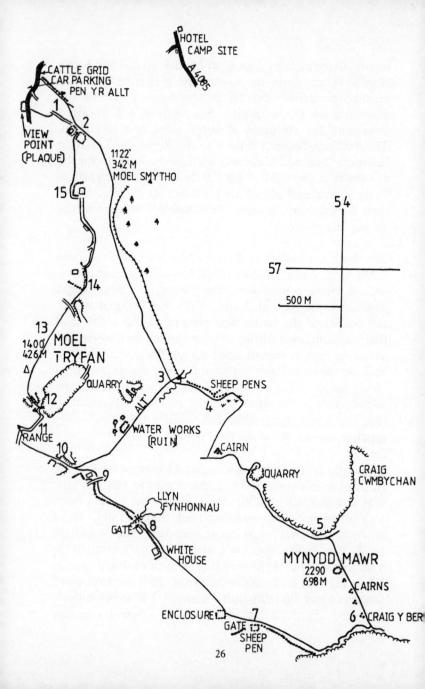

HOTEL
CAMP SITE
A4085

CATTLE GRID
CAR PARKING
PEN YR ALLT
1
2

VIEW
POINT
(PLAQUE)

1122'
342 M
MOEL SMYTHO

15

54

57

500 M

14

13
1400'
426 M
MOEL
TRYFAN
△

QUARRY

3

SHEEP PENS

4

12

ALLT

WATER WORKS
(RUIN)

CAIRN

11
RANGE

10

QUARRY

CRAIG
CWMBYCHAN

9

LLYN
FYNHONNAU

GATE 8

WHITE
HOUSE

5

MYNYDD MAWR
2290'
698 M

CAIRNS

ENCLOSURE
7

6 CRAIG Y BER

GATE
SHEEP
PEN

towards the ridge. Pick up a broad path ascending to a small quarry. Follow ascending path close to the Cwm edge. The path passes a number of deep gullies. **5.** At gully with the most impressive rock formations turn R and head for summit (not in view). From summit descend ridge following cairns. At final cairn continue down to the top of first massive gully. **6.** Go R, at first uphill to follow faint path. Path contours around above crags and then descends ridge line. At wall and fence go R to valley bottom, keeping wall on L. **7.** Pass sheep pen on L and on to gate. Here turn R to look across moor. Path now runs between heather and marsh towards ruined enclosure (low very broken down walls). At enclosure cross open moorland to white farm house, (aim for the summit of Moel Tryfan). At white farm house keep wall on L and head uphill towards slate tips. **8.** Cross stream before ruin and pass ruin to small iron gate. R for 25 metres to wooden bridge and continue following wall line on L. **9.** At wall corner cross track and with ruin close by. Continue uphill and on to top wall corner (one nearest slate tip). Follow faint track 1/2 R towards gap in tip. **10.** Pass between slate walls (ruins). Cross several faint tracks to join main quarry track and turn R. **11.** Pass small bore rifle range on L. Up quarry road. Track turns sharp R before descending into open cast workings. Do not descend track but L at small cairn. **12.** Path ascends a spoil heap and follows faint grassy track up open hillside to summit. **13.** From summit take R/H of two faint paths leading on a bearing of 30 degrees magnetic. Cross track from quarry and follow edge of slate tip down to wall corner. **14.** Follow wall on L down to farm track and R along track. At T junction turn R, continue past houses to rough track. **15.** At cottage at end of track go L and follow wall on R. Continue around wall to second corner and follow on track. Track continues with wall on L initially. When large carpark comes into view cross the heather and then road to inspect the memorial to Kate Roberts. Out of car park and L up road to first car park.

Refreshments The Newborough Arms in Bontnewydd serves good food, or into Caernarfon for the many cafes and pubs.

THE BIG DIPPER

Maps 1:50,000 Sheet 115 Caernarfon and Bangor or 1:25,000 Sheet 17 Snowdon and Conwy
Distance 12 miles / 19.5 Kilometres
Height gained 3560ft / 1085metres
Duration 7 Hours
Terrain High mountain tops
Car park A small car park can be located by turning right 100 metres S.E. after the Snowdon Mountain Railway station and opposite the Royal Victoria Hotel. G.R. 582596

This excursion must be one of the unsung classics of North Wales. In its early stages tumbling waterfalls and the Mountain Railway are followed, later passing through farmland and onto the flanks of Moel Eilio. Concrete bases once used for the foundations of radio masts will be observed high up on the flanks of Moel Eilio. These radio masts were used by Marconi in his early experimental transmissions to Australia. The first signal was transmitted on the 22 September 1918.

The ridge divides the valleys of Llanberis and Betws Garmon, and provides views of Llyn Cwellyn and the Nantlle Ridge. Further along the secluded hollows of Cwm Clogwyn and Cwm Brwynog can be observed.

The line of the ridge climbs and dips over summits and passes, crossing the ancient burial road from Llanberis to Rhyd Ddu before finally joining the Snowdon Ranger path and the final pull up to the summit of Snowdon. Snowdon, *Yr Wyddfa* is the highest mountain in England and Wales and is formed of Ordovician volcanic rock some 4 million years old. On the summit is the "Hotel" from which you may be able to purchase refreshments.

There have been buildings at this location since 1820, when the local guides established a stone built hut to cater for the needs of the many visitors climbing from Llanberis. 1890 saw the opening of a wooden hut which was known as "The Roberts and Owens bazaar". This provided beds and refreshment for the Victorian holiday makers. The first hotel to be owned by the Railway Co. was built in 1897. The present building was constructed in 1934 and as its predecessors had done, it offered accommodation. In 1942 it was occupied by the Air Ministry, the Admiralty and the War Department until the end of hostilities. The building was purchased by the Snowdonia National Park authorities in 1983 with the Railway Company still in the position of offering refreshments but now as lease holders. The building was extensively refurbished in 1988 and is open from late spring to early October.

The world famous railway may never have seen the light of day were it not for the efforts of land owner George Assheton-Smith. In the 1870's the initial attempts to get a scheme off the ground failed. Only in 1894 did a third attempt by Assheton-Smith begin the process of building a railway. It was completed in 14 months and the public opening was in 1896. The first passengers would have paid the princely sum of 5 shillings for this trip and many were keen to sample the excursion. This first trip was unfortunately marred by the only serious accident and fatality to have affected the line. Two trains, one following soon after the other had successfully reached the summit station. On the descent, however, the lead train mounted the track and ran out of control. Near to the present Clogwyn station the train left the track and plunged down the mountain side close to an ascending group of mountaineers. The second train, unaware of the accident crashed into the rear of the now empty carriages.

Incredibly, the only injury in this whole incident was a passenger who leapt from the moving train and broke both legs. He later died in hospital from these injuries.

Cwm Hetiau (Valley of the Hats) is located near Clogwyn station, this Cwm received its peculiar name from the effect it had on Victorian head dress. When the Victorian passengers alighted from the train to look at the spectacular view, their head gear was whipped away by the strong winds into Cwm Hetiau. Later these hats were retrieved by the locals. The head gear was then paraded round the villages for all to admire.

The walk **1.** Turn R out of the car park and along road. Turn R under railway bridge passing playing field on R. **2.** Turn L over cattle grid and up steep lane. After viewing the falls (cross railway track to do so) take a R fork and continue along tarred track to pass between cottages. After what appears to be a dead end, facing the gable end of small outbuildings go R into field and then L with outbuilding wall on your L. Continue on to sheet steel gate in wall. L through gate and across field for 50 metres then R to kissing gates. **3.** Down road for 150 metres then L up to stile and up rough track with wall on your right. Over stile and on to cottages, along the track to join road. **4.** Up the road to its top gate, over stile and L along track and over next stile. Continue for 25 metres then L up faint path. **5.** Soon follow ridge crest to join broad path, later with fence on R. Over stile to summit. Return to stile then R keeping fence and steep ground on your L. Continue along ridge line and on to Foel Goch passing fence edge on R, on to stile. Follow fence on R to track (Bwlch Maes Gwm). **6.** Over stile and up keeping wall and later fence on L. Over Moel Cynghorion and down to meet the Snowdon Ranger path. **7.** Up to meet the Railway track and the Llanberis path up to the summit of

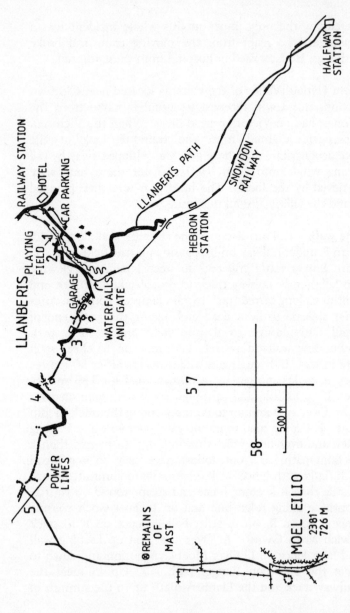

LLANBERIS

RAILWAY STATION
HOTEL
PLAYING FIELD
CAR PARKING
1
2
GARAGE
WATERFALLS AND GATE
3
4
5
POWER LINES
⊗ REMAINS OF MAST
LLANBERIS PATH
SNOWDON RAILWAY
HEBRON STATION
HALFWAY STATION
MOEL EILIO
2381'
726 M

57   58

500 M

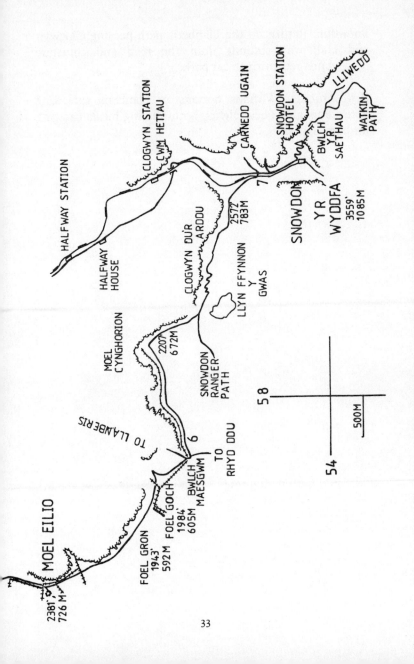

HALFWAY STATION

CLOGWYN STATION
CWM HETIAU

CARNEDD UGAIN

SNOWDON STATION
HOTEL

LLIWEDD

BWLCH
YR
SAETHAU

WATKIN
PATH

HALFWAY
HOUSE

CLOGWYN DU'R
ARDDU

2572'
783M

7

SNOWDON
YR
WYDDFA

3559'
1085M

MOEL CYNGHORION

2207'
672M

LLYN FFYNNON
Y
GWAS

SNOWDON
RANGER
PATH

TO LLANBERIS

6

BWLCH
MAESGWM

TO
RHYD DDU

MOEL EILIO

FOEL GRON
1943'
592M

FOEL GOCH
1984'
605M

2381'
726 M

58

54

500M

33

Snowdon. Return on the Llanberis path passing Clogwyn and Half way stations. Join the road and continue downwards returning to car park.

Refreshments   Various options in Llanberis including Pete's Eats and The Heights, both offering meals catering for large appetites.

CWM CYWION AND THE LLYMLLWYD RIDGE
OF Y GARN

Maps 1:50,000 Sheet 115 Caernarfon and Bangor or
1:25,000 Sheet 17 Snowdon and Conwy
Distance 5 Miles/8 Kilometres
Height gained 3100ft/950metres
Duration 4 hours
Terrain It can be wet into Cwm Cywion but good after
that.
Car park Situated at the west end of Llyn Ogwen near the
Idwal Youth Hostel. G.R.649604

This walk takes you into one of the few secluded cwms
within the northern end of the Glyders. High up in the
cwm, the remains of an aircraft engine may still be found.
The engine type is a double wasp radial and came from an
American aircraft known as a Martin B26 Marauder. On a
transit flight, this aircraft was blown off course and whilst
in thick cloud flew into the side of Y Garn. This happened
on the 1st of February 1945, and sadly there were no
survivors.

There are views across to the broken flanks of Braich Tŷ
Du, the northern Carneddau and across to the Menai
Straits and Anglesey. The Llymllwyd ridge brings the
walker onto the main ridge at Bwlch Cywion. Those
wishing to extend the walk could easily take in the
summit of Foel Goch from this point before heading for
the summit of Y Garn itself. There is a choice of descent
routes from the summit. One is to return to the north
ridge of Y Garn where a steep descent reaches Llyn Clyd.
Here impressive gullies rising steeply back to the summit
of Y Garn can be seen. These are popular as winter climbs
for beginners and experts alike and account for the good
path (known as the fishermans path) which reaches Llyn

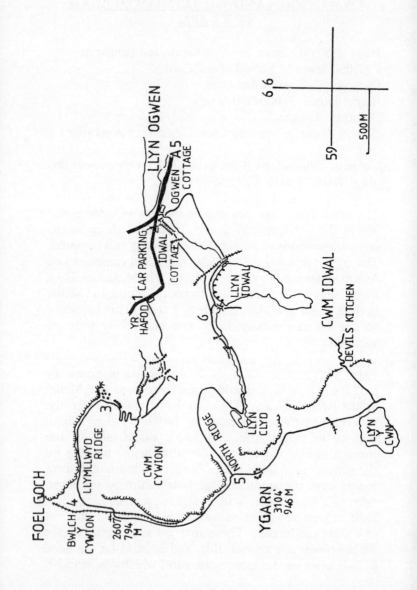

Clyd from Llyn Idwal. Alternatively continue down to Llyn y Cŵn where the path descends via the Devils kitchen.

A descent from Cwm Clyd via the fisherman's path brings the walker down to Llyn Idwal, once called the wildest and most savage lake in Wales. Unfortunately a sad legend surrounds the lake. A young prince, known as Idwal, was out hunting with an envious step father called Nefydd Hardd. The Prince Idwal had been staying with his uncle for some time and had spent much of this time in the company of the uncles own son. Of the two boys, Idwal was by far the most intelligent and showed aptitude for the skills of hunting and riding. He was more athlectic and in many ways represented the type of son Nefydd Hardd would have liked. In order to stop his own son from being shown up, a cruel plan was devised. Whilst out on a hunting trip the young prince was slain and his body disposed of in the lake. The tale now tells us that the lake, because of the evil deed, is now the haunt of demons and that its water has so fatal an effect that no bird flies over or alights on its surface.

Descent via Llyn y Cŵn bring us to another fearsome spectre. High in the face of Cwm Idwal is the Devils kitchen. This dark recess, was feared by mariners entering the port of Penrhyn due to the belief that the Devil was in his lair blowing an offshore wind making entry into the port difficult.

From Cwm Idwal a further choice of paths can be made. The main path being along the shore, over the wooden bridge and through the Idwal gate to return to the car park. Alternatively branch left by the beach and climb a hillock to descend across open moorland to Tin Can

Gully. It was named after the rubbish that built up here in the days before refuse collection took place in the upper Ogwen valley. The gully also had an earlier use when it was the hone stone quarry for the local Penrhyn quarries. Hone stone is a hard stone used to sharpen tools and knives. It was considered to be one of the finest hone stones available in the world and was exported as far as America. It was also used for the supply of classroom writing slates. The quarry was opened in 1796.

The walk Walk L out of the carpark, past the Youth Hostel. Over the cattle grid and down the road for 500 metres to Hafod (Welsh Scout association hut). **1.** L into the car park and across to faint path. Follow this faint path uphill to lip of Cwm Cywion and to the left of the stream outfall of the cwm. Over stile in fence and continue upwards following small stream. Pass remains of old metal fence corner posts. **2.** Through gap in boundary wall. Here go 1/2 R for 200 metres to join faint path from Cwm Idwal. Drop into a small gorge and over stepping stones to zig zag path ascending the side of the scree slope bearing R. Up path and continue diagonally across the flanks of Llymllwyd keeping old wall on R. **3.** At boulder stream ascend to ridge crest, continue on ridge passing sandstone scar. Cross plateau to the fence. **4.** Turn L keeping fence on R. Cross fence at stile and continue along fence. Follow path upwards to the summit to Y Garn. (One descent route carries on to Llyn y Cŵn). Return for 200 metres and then R to the North ridge (extreme care must be taken in poor conditions). **5.** Down steep ridge and L to Llyn Clyd. At Llyn Clyd pick up the outfall and descend the L bank, the path later crossing to R bank. When the stream levels out cross to small rock buttress, here the path is evident. Through wall gap and down to beach. **6.** Along beach, across bridge and L through gate and down path to car park.

Alternative 6. At beach L to fence, over stile and down moorland path to fence. Over stile and descend into old quarry. Through quarry , over stile and into car park.

Refreshments Ogwen falls tea bar (in the car park). Whilst sipping your tea remember that the tea bar here was for those who had come to see the falls. So, walk a short way down the A5 and descend under the road bridge to view the falls and admire the old drovers bridge now hidden from the view of the casual observer.

THE AFONYDD LLAFAR AND CASEG HORSESHOE

Maps 1:50,000 Sheet 115 Caernarfon and Bangor or
1:25,000 Sheet 17 Snowdon and Conwy
Distance 10 miles/16 Kilometres
Height gained 2500ft/760metres
Duration 7 Hours
Terrain Wet just after start, later good hard but care must
be taken between Yr Arig and Bera Bach and Mawr, wet in
patches.
Car park In small off road space just past the village of
Gerlan and its post office or with care on the road side.
G.R. 634662.

This walk involves a scramble section on the spur
running from the apex of Llech Ddu to the flanks of
Carnedd Dafydd. The scramble is of a straight forward
nature but should not be undertaken by anyone who is
not happy with scrambling in the Snowdonia area. An
alternative can be found where the footpath crosses the
base of Mynydd Ddu (the spur from Carnedd Dafydd).
Follow the ascending path, keeping the crags on the left,
to the summit. However, as the scramble provides one of
the highlights of the walk, save the walk for when you
have the experience to enjoy it. The walk follows the
Afon Llafar on a gradually ascending path towards the
impressive massif of Ysgolion Duon (Black Ladders). This
crag being north facing attracts the first winter snows and
is well known as a playground for winter climbers. The
path disappears close to a large boulder field at the base of
Llech Ddu, an imposing triangular shaped crag with a
quartz band at its apex. A faint path ascends to the right
of the crag and then crosses grassy ledges to this quartz
band. Here is the start of the scramble route up Crib Lem.

Carnedd Dafydd is reputed to be the final resting place of Prince Dafydd, who was executed by Edward 1st in Shrewsbury in 1283. Dafydds brother Llywelyn is also commemorated in these hills, both Princes giving their names to the two highest peaks in the Carneddi. Llywelyn ab Gruffydd, was killed in 1282 at the hands of Adam de Francton for refusing to pay homage to Edward 1st.

Carnedd Llywelyn is linked with Mount Kilimanjaro in Africa, Mount Tallac in northern California, the Old Man of Coniston in the Lake District and Le Nid d'Aigle in the French Alps. The link is a curious one and is because in 1960 a religious sect from Los Angeles declared it one of the worlds nineteen Holy mountains and charged with cosmic powers. Anybody ascending the charged rocks at the summit will receive cosmic energies which will help to give enlightenment and unselfish service to mankind.

The walk continues across to the plateau of Foel Grach with its refuge. Twelve slabs of rock have been placed in a vertical position and these can be followed across the ridge to aid the walker in the location of the refuge. The refuge was constructed by local mountaineers who realised the need for a sturdy building in such a remote spot. The original building was constructed in 1964, unfortunately so called mountain lovers had seen fit to deface this sanctuary in such a way that the National Park staff decided to remove the refuge. In 1988 the roof, shutters and door were removed. This resulted in an outcry and a workmans hut was positioned within the walls. The refuge was later returned to its former glory so please ensure that this refuge is kept clean for future use.

The walk continues over the summit of Yr Aryg and then on towards Bera Bach and Bera Mawr. The purist may

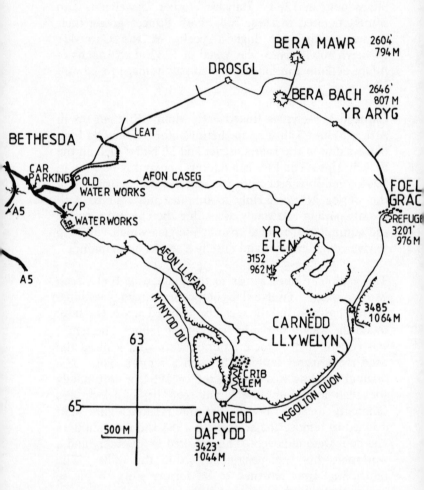

BERA MAWR 2604' 794 M

DROSGL

BERA BACH 2646' 807 M

YR ARYG

BETHESDA

LEAT

CAR PARKING

OLD WATER WORKS

AFON CASEG

A5

C/P WATERWORKS

FOEL GRAC 3201' 976 M

REFUGE

YR ELEN 3152' 962 M

A5

AFON LLAFAR

MYNYDD DU

3485' 1064 M

CARNEDD LL.YWELYN

63

CRIB LEM

65

YSGOLION DUON

500 M

CARNEDD DAFYDD 3423' 1044M

wish to make the detour to gain the summit of Bera Mawr. It is worth pointing out that in this case the words Bach (small) and Mawr (large) appear to be the wrong way round, for it is undoubtedly the case that Bera Mawr at 2606ft/794m is of lesser stature than Bera Bach at 2646ft/807m. None the less the summit of Bera Mawr is worth the effort.

On the walk over to Gyrn Wigau, spend some time looking into the huge bowl of Cwm Caseg. The name means 'valley of the mare', and it is still home to the sturdy Welsh mountain ponies.

The walk Walk along the minor road, over the bridge, to its termination at the new water works. Over stile at right of gate and on with fence on L. **1.** Follow path onto moorland, vague over wet area, but soon becomes clear. **2.** If the alternative to the scramble is required, ascend the spur on L to the summit of Carnedd Dafydd. Otherwise continue along gently ascending path on R of Afon Llafar. The path runs to the base of a large dark crag and an area of huge boulders and sheep pens. **3.** Ascend path at R/H side of crag into small cwm. **4.** Cross grassy ledges, trending L to reach quartz band and apex of crag. Scramble up to summit of Carnedd Dafydd. **5.** L along ridge, narrow later, and up to summit of Carnedd Llywelyn. On to Foel Grach (with its refuge hut) and continue on to Garnedd Uchaf (large pile of stones). Here the ridge splits, with one spur running NE, whilst you require the spur running NW towards Yr Aryg. **6.** Follow this ridge NW to gain the summit of Bera Bach (and Bera Mawr if required). Down ridge, now beginning to trend W and later SW, passing over old leat to Gyrn Wigau. The main ridge continues on to Drosgl and has a clear track. The route to Gyrn Wigau leaves this main ridge and goes down to a small col then on to the subsiduary summit.

Over the summit and down to wall. **7.** Over stile and 1/2 L to track in valley. Along track, with wall on L to gate (sheep pens). **8.** Down lane to T junction and R to carpark.

Refreshments Those with an interest in the curious may be persuaded to take a pint in the Douglas Arms. Unlike other pubs in the book, no bar meals will be on offer here.

This pub, run by the Davies family has ignored decimalisation and still deals in pounds, shillings and pence. The pub itself shows no trappings of modernisation and must be one of the few in the area to still have a full size billiard table. The game of snooker played here uses two extra balls to the standard, a purple and orange.

Cafes come and go in Bethesda and rarely have we found ourselves stopping here. This may be somewhat unfair to establishments in Bethesda and you may wish to investigate for yourself. Otherwise cafes will be found in Bangor or go and pay a visit to the Ogwen tea bar at Idwal.

TRYFAN'S EASTERN TRAVERSE

Maps 1:50,000 Sheet 115 Caernarfon and Bangor or
1:25,000 Sheet 17 Snowdon and Conwy
Distance 3Miles/5 Kilometres
Height gained 1977ft/603metres
Duration 4.5 Hours
Terrain Good and firm on rock, some wet patches in
Cwm Tryfan.
Car park On roadside of A5 at G.R.674604

There is no doubt that Tryfan (Three Peaks) is an impressive mountain, with its steep and fearsome crags and rough overall appearance. Its name has been ascribed to various possibilities. Some have said it reflects the form of the mountain, whilst others say that at one time three 10ft monoliths stood on the summit. Only two monoliths stand there now and the fact that from the road these appear to be two people has given rise to names for the stones. Adam and Eve, Jack and Jill, and Siôn and Siân have been used to describe these two. You may pick your own. Further folk lore concerns those people whose first time it is up Tryfan. In order to gain the freedom of Tryfan it is necessary to leap across the exposed gap from one to the other. The authors would suggest that this be left entirely up to the judgement of the individual.

The popularity of the mountain also led to a less complimentary title. That of the highest dustbin in Wales. Thanks to voluntary groups the summit has been improved considerably. However always remember that you can help by clearing up any litter you may find on this or any other walk. One unfortunate consequence of the clean up was the end of the highest habitation of mice in Wales.

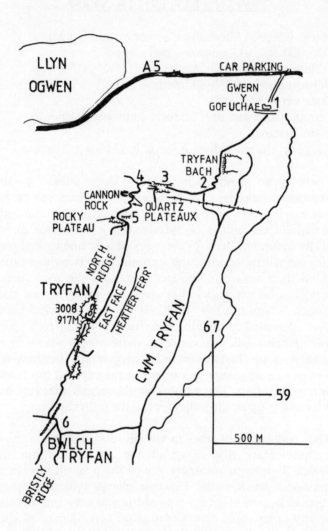

LLYN OGWEN

A 5

CAR PARKING

GWERN Y GOF UCHAF 1

TRYFAN BACH 2

4 3

CANNON ROCK

QUARTZ PLATEAUX

ROCKY PLATEAU 5

NORTH RIDGE

TRYFAN

3008 917M

EAST FACE

HEATHER TERR'

CWM TRYFAN

67

59

500 M

6

BWLCH TRYFAN

BRISTLY RIDGE

Tryfan is also said to be the only true mountain in Wales as it requires the use of hands on some parts of all the ascent routes. This apparently is not the case on any other Welsh Mountain. This excursion is for the more adventurous and should only be undertaken by those with experience of scrambling.

The walk Follow the farm track to Gwern Gof Uchaf and pass to the L and behind farm. **1.** Cross two stiles (and Drovers road). Pass large slab on your L (Tryfan Bach) and continue upwards through gully. **2.** At fence go R and follow fence. Take small path running parallel to fence which then goes R and meets a path rising from the R. **3.** Enter steep gully keeping to the R hand wall. Continue up to the heather covered plateau. **4.** From the heather plateau up over loose boulders and small rock outcrops until the first quartz covered plateau is gained. (From here a short diversion towards Idwal lake will bring you to the rock feature known as the Cannon). Continue up to a second quartz plateau and on to a third rocky plateau with an apparently blank wall in front. **5.** L down gully for 10 metres (Nor Nor gully) and pick up ascending line of the eastern traverse. This line ascends gently in comparison to North Ridge route which ascends steeply. Up and through quartz covered notch, then short descent to the R. Continue along small path and negotiate an awkward step. Ascend grassy ledges to second quartz notch. Here you pass below the summit and a traverse R will bring you to Adam and Eve. Continue to the South summit and then down, keeping as close to the ridge line as possible. Pass wall with two stiles and over rocky outcrop to gain next wall with six stiles. Cross at stile 5 close to large cairn. This is Bwlch Tryfan. **6.** L over stile and passing cairn go 1/2 L to pick up faint path descending into valley. Down path to fence. **7.** Over fence and down valley to farm and parking. Both stiles at the fence will return the walker to the farm but by slightly different routes.

Refreshments For many years the Ogwen Falls Tea bar (in the car park by the youth hostel) has provided a unique service to the walker in this area and no walk in the area would be complete without a cuppa at the Brew shack. Give our regards to Dennis and Anne Johnston.

CWM PENMACHNO SOUTH EASTERN SKYLINE

Maps 1:50,000 Sheet 115 Snowdon and Sheet 124
Dolgellau or 1:25,000 Sheet 18 Harlech and Bala.
Distance 7 Miles/11 Kilometres
Height gained 1265ft/385metres
Duration 5 Hours
Terrain Quarry areas good and dry. Up to plateau, damp
and with much heather. Across to quarry road very wet.
Car park Along side slate spoil heap near the village of
Cwm Penmachno just prior to a sharp bend G.R. 753473.

The road into the village of Penmachno follows the river
Machno as it winds its way along the bottom of a broad
valley. In the village itself is a 6 arched bridge built in
1785 by a local builder, Henry Parry. It is still the main
crossing point of the river

Near to Penmachno a grave stone was found inscribed
with the words "Carausius lies here in this heap of
stones". This stone was erected in memory of a King
Carausius, who according to some historians may have
been the founder of the British Navy. Acting on behalf of
his Roman employers, he built a navy whose
responsibility was to put down the pirates who infested
the waters around the British Isles. So successful were his
exploits that the seas from the Rhine to the Straits of
Gibraltar were cleared of these enemies. He was so
popular with his employers that coins were minted to
commemorate his success. These coins bearing his image
and name have been found on the slopes of the Little
Orme. His name has also been found in the writings of
Celtic Bards, who referred to him as "Mighty Caras King
of Ships".

On gaining the high ground of the walk it is possible to

see Llyn Conwy. This 100 acre lake is the source of the River Conwy and has always enjoyed a reputation for the excellence of its game and fishing. During the period when the lake was looked after by the Penrhyn Estate, it was so successful that fishing club records show one party, during the summer of 1880 catching 111 trout in two days. Unfortunately its success led to poaching on a grand scale. Poaching was so rife that spiked stakes were erected in the lake to prevent the use of Otter boards. These boards were an illegal form of fishing using a board with a number of hooks attached to it which was allowed to drift across the lake with the assistance of the wind and controlled by the use of lines held at the shore. Hefty fines of up to £1:15/6 would have been imposed in the late 1800's to try and prevent the poaching. With the new salmon ladder having been installed under the Conwy falls it is hoped that the upper Conwy and the Conwy lake itself will again become the breeding ground of salmon in the not too distant future.

Tradition tells us that the lake was once owned by the Knights of the order of St John of Jerusalem. The Knights set up a hospice (a house of rest) in nearby Ysbyty Ifan. The Knights gave food and shelter to aid the travellers who passed this way. However in the 14th Century the order was abolished and the hospice became a haven for robbers. These rogues caused much trouble in the area and it became necessary for the local tenants to call on the help of a Welsh chieftain, Meredudd ab Ifan to rid the area of these pests.

Later on in the walk the track of Sarn Helen is crossed as it runs from Cwm Penamnen to Tomen y Mur. Romantic legend tells us that the Deputy Roman Emperor, Magnus Clemens Maximus, whilst stationed in Caernarfon (Segontium) had a dream. In this dream he met, courted and married the incredibly beautiful Princess Elen. In the dream, the beautiful Elen persuaded her husband to construct a road to link the countrymen of North and South Wales. This road was to run from Caernarfon (Segontium) in the North to Carmarthen (Moridunum) in the South. The fact is that the garrison commander from Caerhun (Canovium) in the Conwy valley did marry a Celtic beauty who was called Elen. The remains of this route can still be seen and walked upon, occasionally in the form of a raised paved way. This route is know known as Sarn Helen (The road of Princess Elen).

The walk Through gate (walking man sign) and up quarry road. Follow the track around inclines and up hill until a stile and gate are reached near to the top of the slope. **1.** Over stile and continue up track to ruined dam. Descend to dam and cross stream. At end of dam, L along path, at first running downhill. At old railway tracks (crossing stream) turn R ascending hillside. Path drops to and ascends by side of fence line kept on L. **2.** At end of fence and path continue up hillside keeping stream on L. FROM THIS POINT TO THE SUMMIT OF CLOCHDY PATHS DO NOT EXIST, CARE TO BE TAKEN. Continue uphill when fence turns L, do not follow the fence. **3.** On reaching the plateau ascend rocky spur R. Walk on a bearing of 232 degrees Mag. to old wall, which is low, short and not easily spotted. Follow this and ascend to the summit of Y Frith Craig. Continue along ridge crest. **4.** After Lyn y Gors, drop down to the head of a scree sided valley running to the R and up on to the continuing main ridge line. A vague path appears on the ridge crest. The path runs to the summit of Y Clochdy and along to the summit of Craig Goch before descending to pass around small hillocks. **5.** Immediately after the hillocks (lowest point on the ridge), R along a path marked by wooden stakes. **6.** On small plateau 100

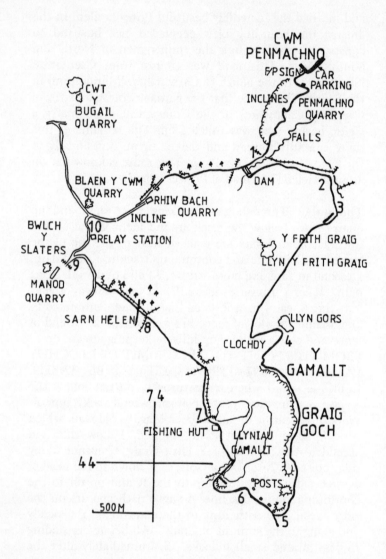

CWM
PENMACHNO

CWT
Y
BUGAIL
QUARRY

F/P SIGN
CAR
PARKING

INCLINES
PENMACHNO
QUARRY

FALLS

BLAEN Y CWM
QUARRY

RHIW BACH
QUARRY

DAM

INCLINE

10

RELAY STATION

BWLCH
Y
SLATERS

9

MANOD
QUARRY

SARN HELEN

8

Y FRITH GRAIG

LLYN Y FRITH GRAIG

LLYN GORS

CLOCHDY

4

Y
GAMALLT

GRAIG
GOCH

7 4

7

FISHING HUT

LLYNIAU
GAMALLT

4 4

500M

POSTS

6

5

52

metres before the lake aim for the L/H edge of the lake. Skirt round this to wall. Pass through the gate and follow fence to lake edge. L over pipe bridge continuing along grassy path down to hut. **7.** Pass the hut and cross to a wall gap (50 metres from waters edge). Through wall gap and 1/2 R to fence. Keep fence on R up to corner. At corner step over fence (with care, gap has been wired up). Continue uphill, in the same direction you have been walking, ignoring the change in direction of fence. Pass small crag on R and when visible, head towards forest corner over wet area. **8.** Over stile and cross "Sarn Helen" (do not enter forest). At fence corner (shallow angle) cross to quarry road. **9.** R up quarry road to entrance gates, sharp R along lower track. **10.** At track junction (just after relay station) R to top of incline. Descend incline towards buildings, path later runs on L/H bank. Pass L of buildings, over stile and along with fence on L. At slight change of direction of fence pass between buildings and down incline to join grassy track. Follow track to parking area.

Refreshments The Machno Arms in Penmachno and Dil's Diner in Betws-y-coed.

CWM BYCHAN'S EASTERN SKYLINE
CLIP, MOEL WION AND RHINOG FAWR

Maps 1:50,000 Sheet 124 Dolgellau or 1:25,000 Sheet 18
Harlech and Bala
Distance 7 Miles/11 Kilometres
Height gained 1600ft/490 metres
Duration 4.5 Hours
Terrain Wet in some places but avoidable by keeping to
ridge line
Car park Situated at the eastern end of Llyn Cwm Bychan
(honesty box). GR645314

This excursion takes the walker into one of wildest and
most remote areas of North Wales, little used except for
the long distance walker travelling between Trawsfynydd
and Barmouth. For the more adventurous motorist an
interesting entry into Cwm Bychan can be made by
turning L in Harlech (opposite the Castle), L at the
Chapel and Telephone kiosk (1.25 Kilometres) then R at
the next turning (1 kilometre).

A good car park and basic camp site will be found at the
eastern end of Llyn Cwm Bychan.

After a short section through upland farmland the walk
soon levels out on to boggy plateau, the path then running
along the screes at the base of Clip to emerge at the
skyline notch. A diversion left will take the walker to the
summit of Clip if time allows. The route follows Boiler
plate rocks of the ridge at first, with no path. A path only
becomes clear after Llyn Tŵr Glas and the crest of Moel
Wion.

The legend of Llyn Morwynion is unfortunately a tragic
one. The legend takes place during the time when the

area of Dyffryn Ardudwy (Harlech) was under the rule of local bandits. The area was also suffering from a lack of females and most of the children being born were males. Three youths who preferred good ale and revelry to fighting were keen to procure wives for themselves. Drinking ale one evening they devised a plan to locate these future brides. Early next morning they set off for the Vale of Clwyd where rumour had it that there were a large number of unattached females. After two days on horseback their search proved successful. Three unsuspecting females were captured, tied up and taken to the youths camp in a secluded part of the Vale. The three captors now had to convince their captives that a good life was awaiting them and that they would be looked after. The journey back began with the three maidens screaming and shouting to be let free but eventually as the homeward passage progressed the girls began to talk to the youths. They told of the boring and strict upbringing they each had and by nightfall had decided that being taken as brides by the youths was not such a bad prospect. That evening they set up camp on the shores of a mountain lake and dreamt of the lives ahead of them.

Next morning as they went to bathe in the lake they saw a terrifying sight. Horsemen charged out of the woods to attack the weaponless youths, who were cut down and hacked to death. The horrified girls recognised the horsemen as their own fathers and brothers. Far from being pleased at being rescued the girls became so distraught that they deliberately drowned themselves in the lake. They had chosen death in preference to life without their new found loved ones. Hence the lake was thereafter called Llyn Morwynion.

Towards the end of the walk the path descends the "Roman Steps" (Bwlch Tyddiad) crossing the well worn

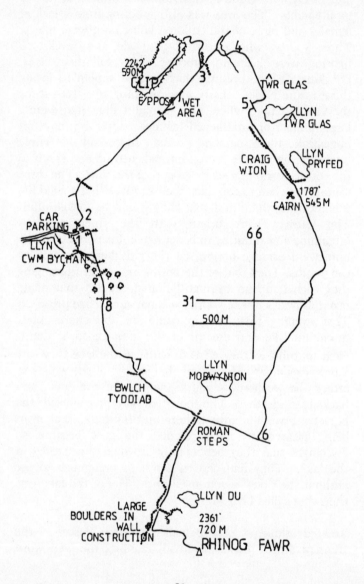

2242'
590 M
CLIP

E/PPOST WET
        AREA

3

4

TWR GLAS

5

LLYN
TWR GLAS

CRAIG
WION

LLYN
PRYFED

CAIRN 1787'
       545 M

CAR
PARKING

2

1

LLYN
CWM BYCHAN

8

66

31

500 M

7

BWLCH
TYDDIAD

LLYN
MORWYNION

ROMAN
STEPS

6

LLYN DU

LARGE
BOULDERS IN
WALL
CONSTRUCTION

2361'
720 M

RHINOG FAWR

slabs.   Sadly it seems that this well crafted path had nothing to do with the Romans despite the nearby Roman road of Sarn Helen less than 4 miles to the east.   It was considered a possibility that the Romans from the fort at Tomen y mur may have used this as a route to the coast. However the more likely explanation for the painstaking work of laying the slabs was to aid the passage of livestock.   The local drovers would have used this upland pass to take the cattle to the market in the border town of Shrewsbury.   This rather less romantic version would appear to have more basis in truth, although as in the case of the story of Beddgelert, its name "The Roman steps" looks likely to remain the one by which it is known.

The walk

Leave Car park R and at farm take sign post for Clip and Bwlch Triddiau. **1.** L over stile. **2.** At white arrow R and on up faint track. Over old wall and on to next arrow (keeping small ridge on L). L at arrow to small notch in ridge (arrow on ridge crest). On to wall with stile and over stile and on along path. Path now runs along the base of the screes of Clip. On reaching boggy plateau aim for the walking man post 15 metres to L to avoid wet path. Head for low point in ridge ahead. ALT FOR CLIP SEE LATER. **3.** Over stile to R of notch and down to small stream. 1/2 R over stream and on to ridge line 60 metres ahead. **4.** Follow ridge crest keeping on boiler plate rocks, no path evident. **5.** At end of initial ridge (just before lake) go R, and cross wet patch to path (15 metres). L up path for 15 metres and fork R to gain next ridge line. L along ridge to wall and where wall meets rocks scramble up to ridge line. Down ridge in southerly direction (path becomes more obvious). Follow level ridge running towards Rhinog Fawr. Path descends steeply through notch in cliff into small valley then climbs steeply to gain ridge again.   Continue through second notch. **6.** Descend to join Roman steps at its highest point. Down to wall with gap (ALT FOR RHINOG FAWR SEE LATER) and through this gap. **7.**Continue down to wall with gate. **8.** Down to wood edge and over stile. Out of wood and over stile keeping wall on L. Over bridge then L over stile and into Car Park.

Alternative to Clip: at notch with wall and stiles (NE end of Clip) do not cross wall. Keep wall on R and keep on to top stile. L up to col, then L to summit keeping to L of ridge line. Return the same way.

Alternative to Rhinog Fawr: At wall with gap L up to notch keeping wall on R. Path swings away from outcrop then at Llyn Du rejoins wall. Path crosses small wall between rocks and crag. Stay on path by wall to top of small rise where large boulders can be seen in wall construction. L to summit. Return the same way.

Refreshments Public houses in Llanbedr but best of all the Plas Cafe in Harlech preferably on a day when you can sit on the terrace.

MOEL Y GEST

Maps 1:50,000 Sheet 124 Dolgellau or 1:25,000 Sheet 18 Harlech and Bala
Distance 4.75miles/7.5Kilometres
Height gained 860ft/262metres
Duration 3.5 Hours
Terrain Good under foot although the summit rocks can be slippery when wet.
Car park In Borth-y-gest village. Good car park and toilets at the top of the beach G.R.565374

This walk starts in the picturesque seaside village of Borth-y-gest, whose claim to fame was its shipbuilding industry in the late 1800's. Indeed the largest sailing ship to be launched in the Porthmadog area was built here. It was the three masted barque "The Pride of Wales". 298 Registered Tons, 125ft long, 26.5ft in the beam and with a draft of 14.5ft. Many of the locals thought that the owner/builder David Morris and the designer Simon Jones were mad, as they believed she was too big to be launched from the site. Fortunately the locals were proved wrong and in 1868 she was successfully launched. For 25 years she plied the worlds oceans carrying cargo before she foundered in a great storm in the North Atlantic in 1892. Between 1826 and 1913, shipbuilding was so important in the area that the 8 yards in existence between Porthmadog and built 260 ships greater than 30 tons in weight. Whilst looking at the many flocks of wading birds in the Estuary, pause to think of these vessels leaving the port with their cargo of slate for delivery any where in the world. For the crews this would be their last glimpse of home for many months.

The walk follows the coastal footpath around the Estuary, where, across the sands can just be seen Sir Clough

Williams Ellis fairy tale village Portmeirion. This Italianate village, with its Bell Tower, Castle, Light House and Waterfront Hotel has for many years attracted visitors as much now for its association with the cult T.V. series the "Prisoner" as for its architectural intrigue.

The Slate industry has been central to the development of Porthmadog but its growth would not have been possible without the foresight of W.A. Madocks. His was the inspiration for much of the early development. In the 1800's land was reclaimed from the Glaslyn estuary and in 1811 a huge embankment known locally as the Cob was built at a cost of £100,000. This enabled an area of 7,000 acres to be reclaimed. Following the completion of the embankment a harbour was constructed thus allowing the establishment of a coastal marine trade. The chief export was Blaenau Ffestiniog slate. The slate was originally brought from the quarries by pack horse, later by horse and cart down to the quays at Maentwrog. Here it was shipped by barges down the river Dwyryd to the estuary where it was trans-shipped to sea going vessels. Following the completion of the Cob it was possible to construct a railway to carry the slates. In 1836 the Ffestiniog Narrow Gauge railway was completed, with a gauge of only 1ft11.5inches. It has unfairly been referred to as the "Toy Railway". The railway was originally horse drawn, with the loaded trucks running down a gradient so skilfully constructed that the slate wagons could be allowed to run down hill themselves for the full 14 miles. The horses having had a free ride down to the port and being refreshed could now haul the empty wagons back to Blaenau Ffestiniog. This system was in use for well over 30 years, until the Ffestiniog railway went over to steam. Two locomotives were built, the "Princess" in London and the "Mountaineer" in New Jersey USA. In January 1865 after two years of only hauling slate, the first passenger service was introduced. It proved so popular that more powerful locomotives were needed. These were to be the double bogie Fairlie patented articulated locomotives (having the appearance of being welded back to back) made by G England and Co. These arrived in 1869, with a further two being built between 1879 and 1886 in the Boston Lodge foundry in Porthmadog. Unfortunately due to the decline of the slate industry the line was closed in 1946 leaving the lines and rolling stock to fall a victim of decay. In 1954 enthusiastic volunteers began the work of restoring the line and in 1955 the first passenger carrying train crossed the Cob. By 1958 trains were arriving at Tan-y-bwlch but it took a further ten years to reach Dduallt. Before Blaenau Ffestiniog could be reached a new tunnel had to be constructed to by pass the Hydro Electric power station. Triumph came at last in May 25 1982 when the first locomotive arrived in Blaenau Ffestiniog after a gap of some 36 years.

The walk Exit car park in top L corner. L along road (Amanda Terrace) and continue along road parallel with coast. Into park and along coastal path (do not descend down to beach). At timber walk way fork R, slightly uphill. At garden fence R up steps to lane. **1.** L down lane. At end of lane continue on path , later with slate wall on R. At end of wall continue onwards. **2.** At lane R for 10 metres then L along path. Path descends steep steps towards golf links. At slipway R and continue along lane towards main road. **3.** L along main road for 150 metres then R across road to entrance to farm track, Glan Morfa Bach Farm. Along track and into farm yard. **4.** Path crosses yard to pass between stables and shed. Over stile and on to wall stile, over wall stile and follow footpath marker under power lines. CARE TO BE TAKEN IN THIS SECTION. Once under power lines

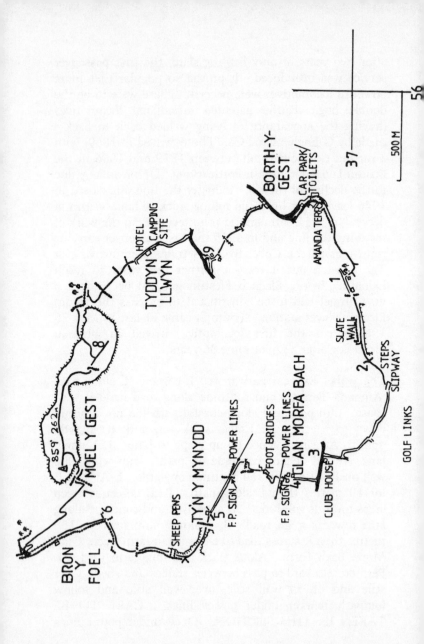

path swings L then R keeping small stream on R. R over slate bridge then L keeping stream on L 25 metres cross stream on timber bridge. Continue upwards towards power lines (the highest pole on the skyline) keeping wall on L. As wall joins rocky outcrop R for 15 metres then L up outcrop . Aim for highest pole. Under power lines to wall corner, wall stile and foot path marker. Over stile and along path to cottage, power lines run parallel with path. **5.** Join track and pass through wall gap to L of cottage Ty'n y Mynydd and continue over stile. Path now runs in small valley and descends through old wall gap to wall gap in new wall (with wooden gate posts). R keeping wall on L and through sheep pens. Continue upwards with wall on L to metal gate and through this. Along grassy track to wall, ascend the track with wall on L to a metal field gate. **6.** L through gate and down to farm Bron y Foel. Through metal field gate and down lane to next metal field gate on R. (If gate is locked follow fence on R. Ascend bank to stile and over stile then R to join zig zags). Up through gate and follow zig zag track. Path continues upwards skirting flank of Moel y Gest, under screes to wall. **7.** At wall L uphill with wall on R. At wall corner R over wall (remains of gate in position). Small path ascends broken ground to ridge. L to summit. Retrace steps then along ridge on crest (various paths) to final summit and viewpoint. Return to wall at col. **8.** 2/3rds R descending down L side of ridge. At wall over stile, through trees and down to col. R. over stile and R along path descending towards caravan park Tyddyn Llwyn. Down to wall gap with wooden posts. 1/2 L down to gate. Continue down to caravan site road, passing hotel on R. Down road to main road and R along main road to lay by (old road). **9.** Cross into lay by and turn L down path and through kissing gate. Continue through a further two gates and into village along sea front to car park

Refreshments Seasonal cafes in Borth-y-gest itself, whilst in Porthmadog the National Milk Bar and the Cafe in the Ffestiniog Railway station provide good food. The Golden Fleece public house in Tremadog (the public houses in the district of Dwyfor only opened on Sundays after the referendum in October 1996) and Eric Jones Cafe under the cliffs of Tremadog (one of the great haunts for climbers).

GYRN GOCH, GYRN DDU THE EIFL
CONTINUATION

Maps 1:50,000 Sheet 123 Llŷn Peninsula or 1:25,000
Sheet 13 Llŷn Peninsula east.
Distance 7 Miles/11 Kilometres
Height gained 900ft/275metres
Duration 4 Hours
Terrain Hard dry moorland
Car park Situated 50 metres South of the Microwave
station above the village of Clynnog G.R.436478

This is a companion walk to the "Eifl walk" and explores
the other side of the range. The territory covered will
allow some unusual and interesting views of Snowdonia
quite different to those normally encountered. Indeed the
mountains as far south as Cader Idris all the way to the
Carneddau will be seen on clear days. Closer to hand Yr
Eifl, its hill fort, the Trefor quarries and the West coast of
Anglesey will provide the foreground. After the initial
steep pull up the walking on the plateau is easy with
plenty to keep the eyes occupied.

The village of Clynnog, which lies at the foot of these
hills, was also the site of a monastery founded in the 6th
century by St Beuno. This monastery later became a
house for Carmelite Friars. Their occupation lasted until
the dissolution of the monasteries in the 16th Century. St
Beuno was also reputedly buried in Clynog, unfortunately
the tomb of St Beuno was destroyed in the 19th Century
and nothing remains to mark the spot. Many stories
surround St Beuno. One tradition states that on the
Saints death a row broke out between the representatives
of the churches of Clynnog Fawr, St Marys of Bardsey
Island and Nefyn. The row concerned which of them had
the right to bury the Saint. Tradition has it that "a deep

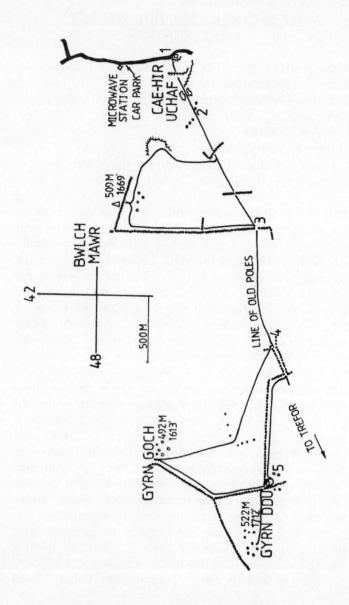

MICROWAVE STATION CAR PARK

CAE-HIR UCHAF

BWLCH MAWR

△ 509M 1669'

LINE OF OLD POLES

TO TREFOR

GYRN GOCH
○ 492M
1613'

522M
1712'
GYRN DDU

42

48

500M

1
2
3
4
5

66

sleep fell on them all and when they awoke three coffins were found, so all three were satisfied". A further story relating to St Beuno concerns livestock. All calves and lambs born with a split or marked ear were considered to belong to St Beuno. This mark is known as St Beuno's mark or "Nod Beuno". The animals were brought to church as an offering and were sold by the church wardens with the money being put into St Beuno's chest, "Cyff Beuno". This money was used to defray church expenses and for the relief of the poor. The church of St Beuno was one of the resting places for pilgrims on their way to Bardsey Island and therefore the well of St Beuno was much used and famous for its healing powers. Clynnog was and still remains a resting place for those on there way to the tip of the Llŷn Peninsula.

The walk **1.** Walk downhill S for 300 metres to a ruined cottage with stile. Over Stile. Due to lack of good paths a bearing may be of use at this stage, a bearing of 120 degrees magnetic providing the general direction. Across field to stile, L and over 2 plank bridges, R directly uphill and on over next stile. Cross small stream to grassed over spoil heaps and indication of earth works. Up to top of these spoil heaps, then L. **2.** Through gap in old wall, path now becomes more evident. On to stile and continue to next stile. Over this and on to third stile with gate at side. **3.** Path now contours and then gently descends following remains of old telegraph poles. Keep wall on L. **4.** Join track with walls on either side, over stile. Turn R and on up towards summit with cairn. **5.** Pass through wall gap L of summit and on to main summit of Gyrn Ddu. Return to wall gap, through and L keeping wall on L to wall stile in corner. Over stile and carry on with wall on L to summit of Gyrn Goch. Return diagonally across the hillside to wall corner and cross this. On to pass second wall corner on R then to walled track. Turn L and return to wall with stile and gate. Over stile and L to follow wall on L. Cross stile 30ft/10metres R of walled corner. Continue with wall on L to its highest point, then R to summit of Bwlch Mawr. Along ridge and over wall stile and on to Trig point. Return to stile and L steeply down to dip and 1/2 R to pass between two large rocky tops. Down to rejoin path and return to car park.

Refreshments The remote nature of this walk means a drive for any refreshments. Pick one on the way back to your base.

YR EIFL, ITS QUARRIES AND HILL FORT

Maps 1:50,000 Sheet 123 Llŷn Peninsula or 1:25,000
Sheet 13 Llŷn Peninsula east
Distance 5 Miles/8 Kilometres
Height gained 900ft/275 metres
Duration 3 Hours
Terrain Lower hills but rough ground in places
Car park Situated 900metres north of the village of
Llithfaen G.R.353440

The unfrequented tops of Yr Eifl offer magnificent views over the Llŷn Peninsula, Caernarfon Bay and the west coast of Anglesey.

Looking inland towards the mountains a panorama stretching from Snowdon to Cader Idris will test the knowledge with its unusual aspect.

Historical interest in the area covers the more recent Industrial archaeology of the quarries to the Bronze age fortress at Tre'r Ceiri. The imposing quarry of Yr Eifl once exported its product via the jetty in Trefor. This in itself was not unusual as most quarries in the area relied on sea transport to move the goods to a market. However, Yr Eifl quarry transported the stone to the jetty in Trefor by means of an aerial cable way. Eddie Doylerush in his book on Aircraft crashes during WW2 tells of an incident involving this cable. On the 9th of September 1943 an Avro Anson from the No3 Air Gunnery School based at Mona was on a training flight. The pilot was putting the aircraft through its paces near the Eifl quarries and inadvertently clipped the cable with the port wing of the plane. The Anson, now out of control plunged into the sea. Three aircraftmen survived the crash and two tragically died.

Also locally is Nant Gwrtheyrn, an old quarry village now used as a centre for Welsh culture. The centre is involved in the preservation of the Welsh language and offers courses for beginners and academics alike. Nant Gwrtheyrn also has links with Welsh folklore. Its name can be translated as Vortigerns ravine, and is reputed to be the last resting place of Vortigern. His name is always linked with that of Merlin, with whom he had many adventures. One of the most famous was the conflict with the dragons at Dinas Emrys near Beddgelert. In a later conflict Vortigern retreated to Nant Gwrtheryn after a battle with the Jutes under the command of Hengist and Horsa. He was accused of betraying his country to the enemy and came here to die.

Undoubtedly the most important historical feature in the area is the magnificent Bronze age hill fort of Tre'r Ceiri (Village of the Giants). Said to be the largest Bronze age hill fort in the British Isles, the site was in occupation up until A.D. 78. The inner walls enclose an area of about 5 Acres on which are situated over 100 huts. The Cytiau (huts) are situated in groups scattered on the terraces and slopes inside the fort. The huts themselves conform to no particular pattern and can be round, oval, oblong and even rectangular. The walls of the huts were crudely built, being about 4ft thick and 3 to 4ft high. This must have led to very cramped living conditions even where huts had two linked chambers. Archaeologists have found remains on the site which paint a colourful history. Roman, British and Celtic pottery has been found as well porcelain beads from Egypt. The nature of the finds and the location of the site would indicate that the fortress was only occupied during the summer season. The lack of

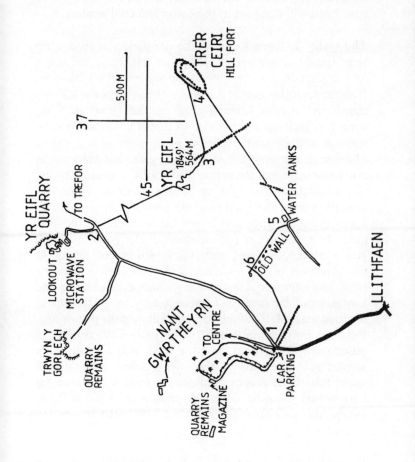

charcoal remains would indicate that fires were not used on the site. This would seem to confirm its use as a summer site, as it is unlikely that the inhabitants would have been without fires in the damp and cold winters.

The walk **1.** Turn R out of the car park and then L up large track towards col. **2.** Just after the top of the rise a gate is seen on the left. One of the summits lies this way. Pass through the gate and towards the microwave station, round the station keeping close to the fence at N.W. corner to pick up and ascend an ancient stairway to the summit and lookout. However as no right of way exists and due to the presence of a locked gate this diversion is not recommended. Return to the col by the same route. Cross track and straight up to the summit. Ignore all crossing tracks and keep to direct path which steepens as it crosses some scree just before the summit. At the Trig point turn to face in the direction of the path by which you ascended. A vague path 1/2 R will be seen going in the direction of Tre'r Ceiri. **3.** Follow this descending track and after initial steep drop go through a wall gap and across moor by means of vague tracks to reach gap in fortified wall. **4.** Through gap and follow path to summit. Descend from summit and follow path S.W. through a different wall gap and on to a stile. Follow path to a second stile and pass to the side of some underground water tanks. **5.** Follow track for 25 metres. Lookout for narrow path running alongside remains of an old wall. **6.** Follow this to a crossing path then L on path and return to car park.

Refreshments Seasonal cafe in Nant Gwrtheyrn, and Cafe and Pub in Llanaelhaearn.

MOEL WINION AND FIVE WAYS

Maps 1:50,000 Sheet 115 Caernarfon and Bangor or
1:25,000 Sheet 17 Snowdon and Conwy.
Distance 6.75 Miles/11 Kilometres
Height gained 1260ft/392metres
Duration 4 Hours
Terrain Good but with some rough moorland.
Car park This is restricted on a minor road adjacent to
Bronydd Isaf Farm and Caerffynnon cottage. Park on the
grass verge ensuring that no passing or turning area are
blocked. G.R.626705

As the walk heads out, views of the majestic Carnedd
Dafydd and Carnedd Llywelyn will dominate the view.
The valleys of Cwm Llafar and Cwm Caseg being the
foreground. The summit in the distance which catches
the eye is the angular summit of Yr Elen. The translation
of the name of this peak varies from Yr Elan (relating to a
young female fawn deer) to Yr Elin (translating as Elbow,
perhaps referring to the shape of a bent elbow). The most
romantic version, however, brings us to a Welsh Princess
known as Elen or Helen. She was also thought to be
linked with the naming of the Roman road Sarn Helen. So
was this particular peak named after a beautiful Welsh
Princess or a bent elbow?

Later on in the walk one of the best views of Aber falls
(Rhaeadr Fawr) will be encountered. These falls plunge for
170ft and the subsequent stream flows out into the Menai
Straits at Abergwyngregyn. Here was one of the last
residences of the Welsh Princes. In the 12th Century,
Llywelyn the Great, built a small wooden castle on a
wooded flat topped mound called Y Mwd. Llywelyn ab
Gruffudd (the last great Welsh leader) also lived here and
was forced into receiving a visit by Edward 1. Being a good

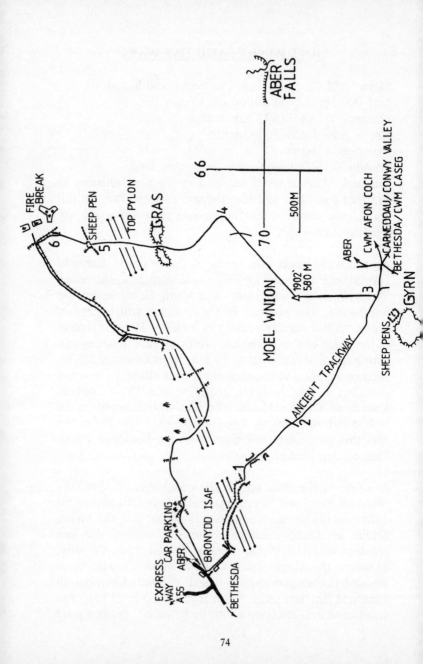

Welsh Prince, Llywelyn refused to pay homage to the English King, who was so enraged that he arranged for the death of Llywelyn at the hands of Adam de Francton in the winter of 1282. His head was paraded through the streets of London to be finally impaled high on the Tower of London. Llywelyn's brother Dafydd also shared an untimely death, hence the names of the two local summits Carnedd Llywelyn and Carnedd Dafydd. Let it be a reminder to those who tread these tops that their names commemorate Welsh Princes who died at the hands of the English.

The walk Over stile and R up track towards Pylons. Through field gate and L up grassy track, keeping wall on R. Follow wall on R under Pylons. Continue along fenced track. Path turns R as it runs between slate fences. **1.** Through gate onto open moorland. 1/3 L and head towards and over small gully in hillock. Pass small quarry on R. Continue up faint track heading towards the summit of Gryn and join ancient trackway. **2.** Continue up and at fork take L hand track. **3.** At saddle and crest of slope, L up to summit (no path). Trig Point on summit. Faint path descends broad ridge (path later disappears) on a bearing of 66 degrees magnetic. As ridge descends Aber falls comes into view. **4.** When the falls are in view turn L heading towards the highest Pylon (far left). Head for vague path becoming more evident as it goes up to a notch in the skyline (passing just left of the top pylon). Continue down path passing under power lines. Head towards fire break in the forest, roughly in the direction of Puffin island. **5.** Through gate and into small sheep pens to exit in the bottom L/H corner of these pens. 1/2 R towards fire break in forest. Down to wall. **6.** At wall corner down L keeping fence on R. Through gate and L along tractor track keeping fence on L. Over stile keeping fence on L.   **7.** Over stile keeping fence on R Under Pylons.   Over at next stile, under Pylons and continue along grassy track to stile.   Continue along this track to start.

Refreshments   The Legend in Penmaenmawr is reasonably close and is popular for food, whilst in Aber itself a small seasonal Cafe will be found.

PENMAENMAWR, THE NORTH EASTERN CARNEDDAU

Maps 1:50,000 Sheet 115 Caernarfon and Bangor or
1:25,000 Sheet 17 Snowdon and Conwy
Distance 6 Miles/10 Kilometres
Height gained 1480ft/451 metres
Duration 3 Hours
Terrain Very good with virtually no bogs
Car park When entering and leaving the village of
Penmaenmawr care must be taken with the junctions on
the A55 expressway. On approaching from the Conwy
direction the access is from the roundabout before
Penmaenmawr. Coming from Bangor, the dual carriage
way splits and follows the old coast road, where the two
roads join again and by one of the tunnels turn
immediately R. Two car parking areas are available, one
at the western end of the village near to Crimea Terrace
where space is available on the roadside. The second area
is close to a church with a tower where the road is
particularly wide. Both these areas lie to the west of the
shops in the village.

It is very difficult in any mountainous area to avoid the
impact that man has had on the environment. Indeed in
this case it is part of the attraction. Some of the impact
dates back to very early inhabitants of the area, whilst the
expressway completed in 1993, has had an impact in that
it provides the ease of access which has brought visitors to
enjoy the walking which the area provides. The early
visitors to the area had to wait until 1772 for the first
road passable by stage coach to be built by the Engineer
Sylvester. Unfortunately there were many accidents due
to the construction methods used on the scree covered
slopes. The road was improved in 1827 by Thomas
Telford, and this method of access was soon to be

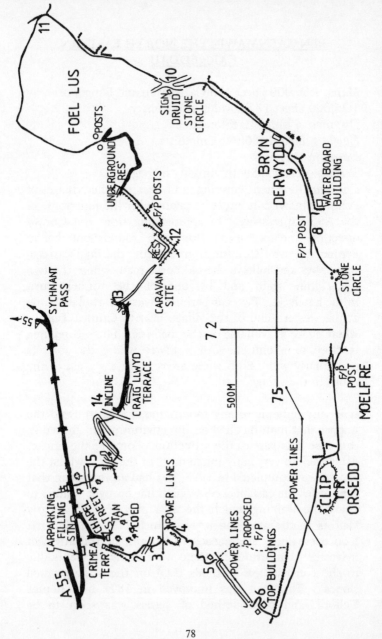

78

followed by the railway constructed by Stephenson. This increased accessibility brought tourists into Penmaenmawr including the then Prime Minister W.E. Gladstone, who in the 1890's was trying to promote the area as a summer resort.

The district contains many relics of ancient times, perhaps the chief of these being the ancient Celtic post of Braich y Dinas, which stands on the conical peak of Dinas Penmaen. The post consisted of a number of circular huts contained within crude stone walls. On the summit of Moelfre is Meini Hirion. Here 10 upright stones set in a circle, with smaller stones in-between, mark a site of importance to the Druids. The site may have had religious significance or may have marked a burial site for a great hero. There is no doubt that standing within the stone circle the site has an imposing feel about it. On the skyline of the walk will be seen Tal y Fan with its pass, Bwlch y Ddeufaen. Here runs the Roman road from Aber to Tal-y-cafn leading eventually to the Roman fort of Canovium, now known as Caerhun. There is so much history in this area that this short account barely scratches the surface. It seems strange that an area with so much history to it should now be amongst the quieter parts of Snowdonia.

The walk Ascend the road opposite the petrol station. Turn R up Chapel St and continue to the top of this road. **1.** At the cottage Tan y Coed go R for 50 metres then L through kissing gate. Take path directly uphill, initially with wall on L, through the edge of the woodland. **2.** At the fork L uphill at a slightly easier gradient. Through sheet steel gate and cross quarry road and continue upwards on left hand path. Diagonally up scree slope on R passing underneath powerlines to the R of an overgrown steel gate. **3.** Turn L passing under power lines and crossing a storage area. **4.** Turn R to ascend L/H ridge of old quarry (Yellow mark on 2nd tree). Follow ridge line up steeply, (sometimes in trough of old pathway or on newer path). Bear L at railway line fence posts. **5.** Up to ruin and follow power lines to quarry road. HERE THE PATH DIRECTION IS DUE TO CHANGE TO TAKE THE WALKER DIRECT TO A STILE UNDER THE SUMMIT OF CLIP Y ORSEDD. THIS WILL AVOID CROSSING THE OPERATIONAL AREA OF THE QUARRY. If at the time of the walk no change is evident continue as directed. Continue along the road with power lines above towards the top buildings. **6.** Through buildings to metal style behind them. Over style and turn L to pass under power lines. Follow broad ridge to wall corner. **7.** 1/2 R to join grassy track then 1/2 L parallel with power lines. Join path coming from R and continue to footpath sign. **8.** 1/2 R up to ridge crest to view stone circle and the Carneddau. Descend to join footpath at footpath sign. After sign and once under power lines track runs along with wall on R. **9.** Track turns R through wall gap and down to a line of trees. At trees turn L along path to pass in front of house (Bryn Derwydd). Through gate and onwards with wall on R. **10.** At track junction (4 tracks) turn R. Where track and wall bear R continue onwards on grassy path. **11.** At path junction 1/2 L on level path (do not descend). At castleated pillars descend road to underground water tank. L through kissing gate keeping fence on R. Follow walking man posts. **12.** At dip in track, opposite reservoir boundary, over stile. Path now skirts reservoir boundary. Continue down to road. **13.** At junction L along road. **14.** At sharp R/H descending bend (after Craig Llwyd terrace) L into walled footpath under quarry incline. Down path to quarry road at bend. Cross road (1/2 L at bend, do not go through kissing gate) small path runs parallel with road. **15.** Cross road and descend down path to buildings. Cross road and through kissing gate. Path descends with wood boundary on L. Descend to road and L to return to car.

Refreshments Penmaenmawr has only a chip shop and is not recommended as a place to stop for refreshments. A return to Bangor or Conwy will provide a much better choice. The tea rooms (Annas) above the climbing shop on Conwy's main street is well worth the effort.

THE LLYN COWLYD CIRCUIT

Maps 1:50,000 Sheet 115 Caernarfon and Bangor or
1:25,000 Sheet 17 Snowdon and Conwy
Distance 7.5Miles/12 Kilometres
Height gained 913ft/278metres
Duration 4.5 Hours
Terrain Mostly good although some areas are very wet.
Notably close to the fence on the ascent of Creigiau
Gleision and during the descent from Bwlch Mignog to
the Leat.
Car park The drive across to the start of this walk is
something of an adventure in itself. In the centre of
Trefriw, opposite the Fairy Falls public house turn up the
minor road. A sign "CEMETERY, MYNWENT" is on the
corner. The road climbs steeply becoming a single track
road with few passing places and in the steepest section
has some severe bends. The road levels out to cross open
moorland and finally drops down to a bridge and gate.
Park here at G.R.744642 at Pont Brwynog.

The lake being one of the deepest in Snowdonia and one
of the least visited is steeped in superstition. One tale
tells of a mythical bull of terrible appearance. It has hoofs
and horns which spurt out fire and nostrils pouring out
steam, and is reported to leap out from the depths at
solitary wanderers with awful consequences. Perhaps a
companion would be advisable for this excursion.

One young man who appears not to have feared meeting
the mythical Bull was Will Roberts. He was employed by
Dolgarrog power station to inspect the pipeline and dam
for damage or acts of sabotage. On 20th February 1944
he was about his usual job when he came across a crashed
Avro Anson aircraft on the hill between Llyn Cowlyd and
Cwm Eigiau. He managed to save three of the crew. The

area in general has had many aircaft crashes and those who wish to learn more would be advised to search out the books of Eddie Doylerush or Roy Sloan.

On the descent from Creigiau Gleision, the walker may well be able to see a quick option to gain the end of Llyn Cowlyd. This way has no landmarks to act as a guide and would be difficult in poor visibility. Secondly the leat only has a limited number of places it can be crossed and none present themselves if this short cut is taken.

The walk 1. L in front of ruin and along track. Over stile below locked gate. 2. At dam, L ascending to left hand corner of the dam and over stile 1/2 L to concrete cairn. Ascend R picking up a track which at first runs up valley as if on a continuation of the dam wall. 3. Path climbs under a small outcrop and then meanders up to the ridge line. Follow path to fence and stile. Do not cross stile. 4. Ascend R following fence to high point and then cross at metal corner supports. 5. Continue along path over subsidiary summits. 6. At summit retrace steps for 25 metres then L. Path descends under rocky outcrops to saddle, keep on ridge line. 7. At final summit, with cairn on top, (Craig Lwyn) R into valley , steep at first. Continue to Moel Ddefaid where another steep descent brings the walker to the Saddle of Bwlch Mignog. 8. Here cross the Bwlch to the edge of Graig Wen, do not ascend. R down open moorland to join stream running to the leat. Keep stream on R, faint path eventually appears. 9. At bridge cross leat and R along leat. 10. Over at stile, then R over leat and along path with fence on R. 11. Cross bridge at leat junction, over ladder stile and down path. This runs parallel but slightly higher than stream. Continue along lake side path. 12. At wall, near dam end of lake, ascend to track, through gateway and along track.

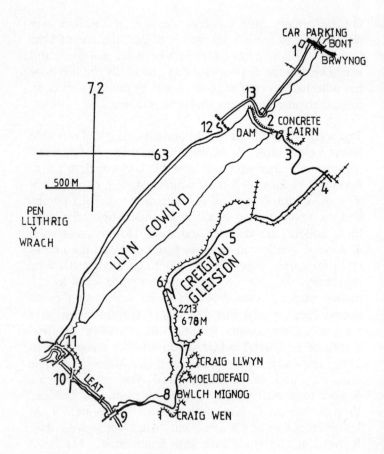

13. At Dam R down track to building then L and return to car park.

Refreshments Return to Trefriw and you have a choice of the Fairy Falls hotel or the cafe Llys Caradog.

MYNYDD TŴR (HOLYHEAD MOUNTAIN), ITS QUARRY AND SIGNAL STATIONS

Maps 1:50,000 Sheet 114 Anglesey or 1:25,000 Sheet 734 Holyhead
Distance 6 Miles/10 Kilometres
Height gained 720ft/220metres
Duration 4 Hours
Terrain Good and hard.
Car park In Holyhead follow signs for the Country Park and just before an old bridge over the road, park in the overspill car park. This is close to the start of the Breakwater. G.R.234835.

This walk starts at a small car park close by the maintenance buildings for the breakwater. Here it is possible to take a small diversion to view the impressive Breakwater. The limestone blocks in the main construction were quarried and transported from Moelfre on Anglesey's Eastern coast. The construction was designed and overseen by James Meadows Rendal. Work began in 1848 and the original design was for a North Breakwater some 5360ft long and an Eastern Breakwater extending from Salt Island. This Eastern Breakwater was to be 2000ft long and to include a Mail packet berth. The whole construction would have given a sheltered anchorage of some 267 acres. In 1854 the plans for two breakwaters was abandoned as it was thought that ships the size of the Great Eastern (some 700ft in length and 20,000 tons in weight) would become the norm, and the existing plans would not have accommodated such vessels. The Northern breakwater was extended by 2000ft then a further 500ft to create a breakwater 7860ft in length and enclosing an area of sheltered water covering 667 acres. The total cost on completion was £1,285,000 and was officially opened on the 19th of August 1873 by Albert Edward "the Prince of Wales".

As the walk continues along the coast, a small cove will come into view, this is Porth Namarch, once the site of the Holyhead Terracotta works. The works exported yellow and red clay for the production of pottery, exporting its goods as far afield as Glasgow. Close inspection of the rocks on the cliff edge show ring bolts used for the purpose of mooring boats whilst they were at the works. These bolts date back to the 1800's.

The footpath to North Stack is the one which was used by donkeys to carry food, gunpowder and supplies from the Trinity House Depot in Holyhead to the Fog Signal Station. This station was constructed in 1857 as a warning system to shipping during foggy conditions. The earliest warning system was shots fired from Naval guns. It wasn't until 1956, with the introduction of electricity to the signal station that the guns were abandoned. The Naval guns were unceremoniously dispatched over the cliffs to land 200ft down on the beach. In 1984 one of the guns was retrieved by members of H.M. Coastguard Cliff Rescue Team and Holyhead Lifeboat Crew. This gun now stands in the country park.

The area between North Stack and South Stack light house is called Gogarth bay, a climbing mecca made popular by famous names such as Joe Brown, Pete Crew and many more. It is still as popular today and walkers may wish to take a small diversion down to the vantage point close to the spectacular Wen Slab. Here it is possible to watch climbers pit their skills against the technical climbs in the area.

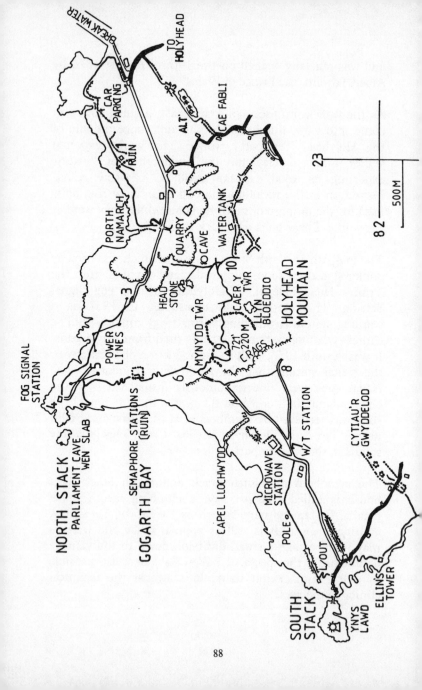

On the subsidiary summit stands the remains of two signal stations. The original being built in the 17th century to communicate with the Packet ships entering and leaving Holyhead. The method of communication was by flags to and from the ships and on to the depot on Salt island. The more recent station was built in the late 1700's due to the increase in sea trade to the port of Liverpool. Merchants and Ship owners felt the need of early news of the arrival of their ships and cargo. Later on it was decided to extend the method of communication by erecting semaphore stations along the Welsh coast. By 1827 a communication network had been set up between Liverpool and Holyhead, a distance of some 70 miles and requiring 12 stations. The operators of the semaphore stations became so expert that Liverpool ship owners would receive information about the arrival of ships off Holyhead in less than a minute. From 1860, the semaphore system was superseded by electrical transmissions, resulting in the closure of intermediate stations and the inevitable loss of jobs.

At South Stack car park, descend the steps towards the lighthouse to admire the unusual rock strata of the area. The lighthouse stands on land owned by the R.S.P.B. and operated as a reserve. The lighthouse here was designed and constructed by Daniel Alexander and began its operational life in 1809. The basic structure has not been changed since, although in 1827 a suspension bridge was built to span the gap between the mainland and the island. Prior to this, visitors had to brave the swirling chasm in a wicker basket hauled along a rope. Electrification of the light came in 1938 and it was automated in 1984. The height of the structure is nearly 200 ft from sea level to the top of the light and the beam of the light can be seen up to 20 miles away. On to the top car park a short descent can be made to Ellins' Tower, which stands on top of 400ft high cliffs. The tower was built between 1820 and 1850 by Lord Stanley of Alderley, as a summer residence for his wife Ellin. The building is now operated by the R.S.P.B. where visitors can observe the seacliff birds in their natural habitat. Birds observed include Storm Petrels, Peregrine Falcons, Great Black Backed Gulls, Common Gulls, Terns, Guillemots and Razorbills.

The walk Over stile (Footpath sign) and along path with boulders on R. Path 1/2 L down to beach. L along top of beach and up steps. Path runs along cliff top with fence on L. **1.** At small ruin on L, take R fork following cliff edge to join quarry road. **2.** R up incline. **3.** Immediately at top of zig zag track, go 1/2 R following telephone poles. **4.** At fog station L uphill. **5.** As track levels and passes under power lines R and soon L. Continue up any of the many paths to the North summit. Pass through walled enclosure (Signal station) and follow path to plateau. **6.** Take R fork up to ridge crest and descend steps to broad track. Track now passes micro wave station. **7.** When track joins tarred road cross this and continue along path which runs along ridge to the Lookout. At Lookout go L descending to car park. L up road to next car park (Top car park). L across car park and out at the back to ridge crest. Along ridge to tarred road and R along road. R fork along track. Close to microwave station take R fork. **8.** At R/H bend in track (close to crags) L up path going uphill. When broad track is reached R up steps to ridge crest and R. Path climbs up through old fort wall to summit. **9.** To descend from summit, track descends towards Breakwater 1/2L. and passes through wall. **10.** At track junction, just above walled enclosures go L descending to pass water tank. Cross road and down footpath to pass between houses and L down road. At sharp R/H bend in main road go L along track. On reaching road go L and continue along this road to its termination (a footpath does run from the farm on the L, "Cae Fabli" to the car park but during the summer it is overgrown and difficult to follow) then R down track. **11.** L through kissing gate and cross field to road to country park. R along road to car park.

Refreshments South Stack Cafe at South Stack car park (seasonal). Otherwise numerous establishments in Holyhead itself. Those returning across Anglesey may wish to stop at the Toll house cafe at the Holyhead end of the Stanley embankment. The Bull Inn in Valley is also a recommended place for meals.

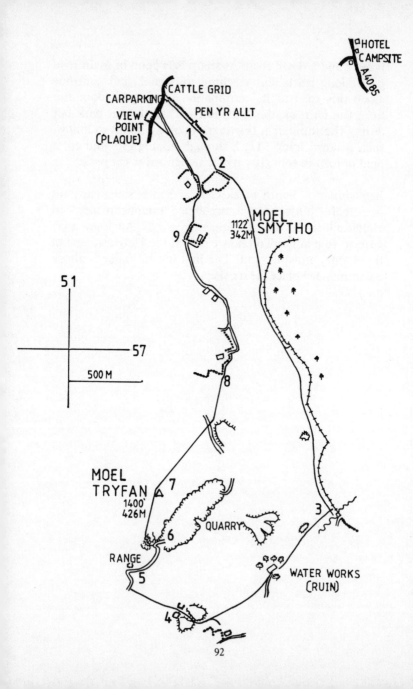

THE KATE ROBERTS WALK

Maps 1:50,000 Sheet 115 Bangor and Caernarfon or
1:25,000 Sheet 17 Snowdon and Conwy
Distance 6.5 Miles/10 Kilometres
Height gained 2320ft/707metres
Duration 3.5 Hours
Terrain Good with very few wet patches.
Car park Easiest when travelling from Caernarfon. After
passing through Waunfawr look for the Snowdonia park
pub on L. 50 metres after this turn R at sign for
Rhosgadfan. Up steep hill and over cattle grid with gate
at side. 150 metres further up park at grassy car park on
R.

THIS VIEW HAS REFRESHED THE SPIRIT OF MANY
AND INSPIRED THE WRITINGS OF KATE ROBERTS
OF RHOSGADFAN 1891-1985. This memorial to Kate
Roberts is erected in the walled car park close to the
Waunfawr to Rhosgadfan road known as *Y Lôn Wen* (the
white road). *Y Lôn Wen* is also the title of one of her
novels. Kate Roberts is well known in Wales for her
novels, short stories and critical judging in the National
Eisteddfods. In between 1925 and 1976 she wrote 16
novels and many short stories about Wales, and the
Welsh way of life. She was born in 1891 into a large
family, in Bryn Gwyrfai near Rhosgadfan. 4½ years later
the family moved to near by Cae'r Gors. In 1904 she won
a Scholarship to the Caernarfon County School where six
years later she passed exams to gain a position in the
University of Wales, Bangor. In 1913 she graduated in
teaching and music. Her first teaching post was close by
in a Llanberis Primary School which then led to a
teaching post in South Wales. 1925 saw the publication of
her first short story *O Gors y Bryniau*. Her marriage in
1928 led to her and her husband moving to Denbigh and

the purchase of a local printing works. This works produced the national paper *Y Faner* on which they both worked. She continued with the running of the printing works after the premature death of her husband in 1946. In 1950 she was made a Doctor of Literature. She retired from *Y Faner* in 1956 to continue with her literary works until her death in 1985.

The walk L out of car park and after 25 metres 1/2 R along track to follow wall on L. **1.** After gate to Penrallt take right hand fork in track. **2.** Along with wall kept on R. From wall corner follow meandering track to top of hill. Head down to wall corner by forest boundary. Follow wall on L. Pass kissing gate on L and on to stream. **3.** At stream turn uphill and follow vague path. Path goes to left of large boulder then at boulder aim for dip to left of slate tip. Head for an old water tank flanked by trees. Follow grassy track onwards to pass right of shallow ponds. Turn R uphill on small grassy path and head for corner of wall nearest to slate tip. Follow faint track right towards and through gap in tip. **4.** Pass between slate walls (ruin). Cross several faint tracks to join main quarry road. **5.** Turn R to pass small bore rifle range on L. **6.** Track turns sharp R before descending into open cast workings (those wishing to explore can do so missing out the summit) and at this point a small cairn marks a path rising up spoil heap. Follow faint grassy path up open hillside to summit. **7.** From the summit take the right hand of the two faint paths leading on a bearing of 30 degrees magnetic. Cross track from quarry and follow edge of slate tip down to wall corner. **8.** Follow wall on L down to farm track. At T junction turn R. Continue past houses to rough track. **9.** At the cottage at the end of track turn L to follow wall on R. Follow wall to second corner and follow on track at far side between walls. Track continues with wall on left at first. When large car park comes into view cross heather and then road to inspect memorial to Kate Roberts. Out of car park and up road to return to start.

Refreshments The choice of where to go from the walk gives many options but a favourite choice would be the Newborough Arms in Bontnewydd and cafes in Caernarfon.

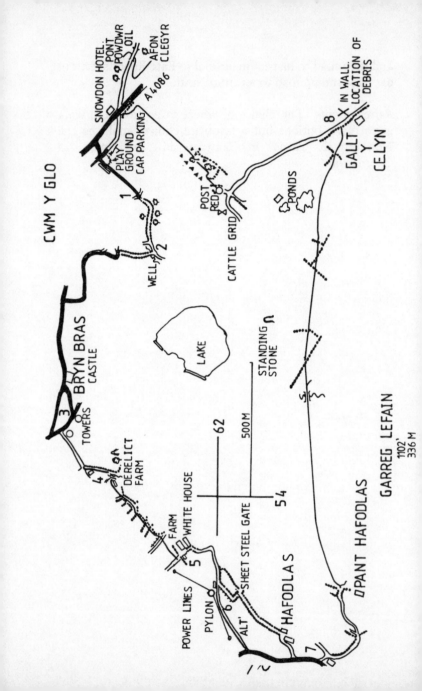

THE POWDWR OIL WALK

Maps 1:50,000 Sheet 115 Caernarfon and Bangor or
1:25,000 Sheet 17 Snowdon and Conwy
Distance 4 miles/6.5 Kilometres
Height gained 860ft/262m
Duration 3 Hours
Terrain Mostly good paths some bracken. The middle
section may have some dense vegetation in summer so
care may be needed to keep to path.
Car park Turn off the A4086 and turn into the village of
Cwm y Glo opposite the "Snowdon" hotel and park
alongside the play ground. G.R. 553625.

This gentle and scenic walk has a historic but tragic note
to it. The walk starts at the village of Cwm y Glo which
was the scene of a massive explosion on the 30th of June
1869. The explosion was caused by Nitro-Glycerine
(Powdr Oil). The actual site of the explosion is on the old
road at a place known as "Gwastad Llyn Coed", in a
cluster of trees behind the Council Highways store. The
explosion, which caused the death of five people and
injured eight, also caused considerable damage to the
Railway station and the new hotel then being built. This
hotel is now called the Snowdon and was one of the first
brick buildings constructed in the area, hence its local
name of "Y Fricsan".

The Nitro-Glycerine was being transported by horse and
cart from the schooner "Heroine" anchored at Aber Menai
Point to storage at the quarries in Llanberis. The two
hauliers had just continued on their journey after a
refreshment stop at the two local Inns, when the incident
happened. The sound of the explosion could be heard as
far away as the north coast of Anglesey and debris was
thrown on to the top road between Bryn Bras and

Llanberis. The real cause of the explosion is still a mystery.

The walk passes the entrance to Bryn Bras castle. Far from being a real castle this is a folly built in the 19th century. The castle and its gardens used to be open to the public, but unfortunately this is no longer the case. It is unlikely that this current state will change. Later in the walk, the views towards Snowdon and the Llanberis pass gradually reveal themselves in a panorama quite unique for such a low level walk.

Detour to the site of explosion Cross the A4086 and turn L between the hotel and highways store, through a gate and along the old road to a cluster of small trees within 15m of the end of the road. Here a small stream passes under the road. This is the Afon Clegyr and the bridge is known as "Pont Powdwr Oil (Nitro-Glycerine Bridge)." Return to the car park.

The Walk Walk towards the village and take 1st L uphill. **1.** At footpath sign continue up enclosed path through wood. Up lane. **2.** At Ornate Well in wall turn R over stream and along enclosed path. Continue along surfaced lane to T junction. L at junction. Continue to next T junction and turn L towards Bryn Bras castle (a folly built in the 19th Century by Thomas Hopper). **3.** Just before the first of two white round towers turn R down lane (footpath sign). Through kissing gate keeping wall on L, as wall turns left undergrowth may be thick. **4.** Over slate bridge and through kissing gate passing in front of derelict barns and cottage. Continue at same level through wall gap to gate. Follow slightly raised path to stone stiles and then a gate. At wall corner cross field on rough track towards a pylon. At track L towards farm. **5.** Cross farm yard to top R.H. corner, through kissing gate and continue up enclosed pathway. At white house through gate R then through road gate to lane. **6.** At road gate just before pylon through kissing gate keeping wall on L and L up to sheet steel gate. *The path can be overgrown at this point and a alternative can be taken. Continue down track to metalled road. Turn left and follow road along until a pillar box is seen in a wall on left. Continue directions from* * *sign.* R along level path. On reaching outbuildings track turns R then L around cottage. Continue down to road. * L up road for 100 metres. **7.** At footpath sign 1/2L over cattle grid. At sharp bend take grassy track going straight on. Over stile and up track. At boundary wall, over stile and 1/2 L up track to moorland. Contour round hillside to join boundary wall. Over stile and 1/2 R on raised pathway. Over stile L crossing marshy field to kissing gate. Raised path crosses a stile and passes through 2 kissing gate before emerging onto road. **8.** *At this point a small detour can be made to 50m R. Here just below a white cottage called Gallt y Celyn a stone in the wall can be found inscribed with a large X. This marks the furthest point where debris from the explosion was located and a stone is provided to maintain the X. Return to the last direction.* L up road to cattle grid. R before cattle grid to pass stone gate post with X marked in red. Pass between next stone posts. Continue down ridge keeping trees on R. Down through bracken again trees on R. R off ridge into gully and down gully. At wall L and take path in bracken running parallel with wall to stile. Cross stile and down to old road.

Refreshments Glyntwrog in Llanrug or to Llanberis and Pete's Eats.

THE LLYN PADARN CIRCUIT

Maps 1:50,000 Sheet 115 Caernarfon and Bangor or
1:25,000 Sheet 17 Snowdon and Conwy
Distance 5.5 Miles/9 Kilometres
Height gained 500ft/152metres
Duration 4 Hours
Terrain Good firm walking although slates on steep
sections require care.
Car park The Lake side car park close to Llanberis
G.R.579605

This low level walk will bring views of Snowdon's
northern cwms, Moel Eilio, the Big Dipper ridge and the
Dinorwig quarries. The latter is the location for the
largest Hydro Electric pumped storage power station in
Europe. The power station is almost entirely contained
within the mountainside of Elidir Fawr in a series of
exceptionally large caverns. Power is generated by water
being released from the top lake, Llyn Marchlyn Mawr, to
run through tunnels in the hillside to turn turbines down
at the level of Llyn Peris. At a moments notice 90,000
gallons of water can be released bringing generators in the
deep caverns up to power. These will generate 1300 Mega
watts of extra electricity for the National Grid, coming to
full power in 10 seconds. At night when the need for
power is reduced the process is reversed and water is
pumped back up to top lake to be ready for the surges in
demand of the National Grid.

The walk starts from the lakeside car park in Llanberis.
The lake, Llyn Padarn was possibly named after Saint
Padarn. It is 90 ft deep and is one of the few lakes in
Snowdonia to be host to the wild Arctic Char. The lake
was also used for sporting events. In 1958 it hosted the
Empire and Commonwealth games rowing competitions.

Royal Spectators were present, as was quite common on these occasions, with the presence of Prince Phillip. He was veiwing the event from a pontoon used by the Umpires when it unfortunaely sank. Being close to the lake shore Prince Phillip suffered nothing more than wet feet, which considering the steep sides of the lake was very fortunate.

The walk follows the lake shore to the dominant Dolbadarn castle, standing on a rocky outcrop between the two lakes. This is one of the few genuine Welsh castles, as the majority of castles in Wales were castles built by the Normans to subdue the Welsh. The original foundations of the castle are so old that no account of them can be found. It is thought it may have been constructed by Maelgwyn Gwynedd in the 6th Century. However references to a castle on this site date to the much later years of 1216 and 1240 when Llywelyn ab Iorwerth was credited with building a castle to command the trade route between the mountains and the rich pasture lands on Anglesey. The castle consists of a round tower which originally had three floors and a dungeon. The castle was to figure strongly in Welsh history and during the wars fought by Owain Glyndŵr it was lost and retaken a number of times. Considering its violent history it is remarkable it has remained in such good condition.

Above the Welsh slate museum towers the Dinorwig Quarry with its labyrinth of tunnels and open cast workings. The names of the workings conjure thoughts of travel world wide with names such as Abysinia, Egypt, Australia and California. Whilst lower down, ladies names Enid, Victoria and Vivian, relate to quarries being named after the owners families. The slate in this area was amongst the best quality to be found and was particularly suitable for flooring, sill, lintels, fireplaces and vats for the

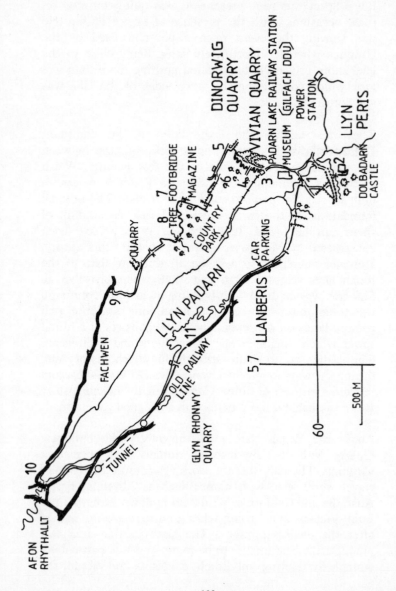

AFON RHYTHALLT

10

FACHWEN

QUARRY

9

8 TREE FOOTBRIDGE 7

MAGAZINE

COUNTRY PARK

6

5

DINORWIG QUARRY

VIVIAN QUARRY

PADARN LAKE RAILWAY STATION

MUSEUM (GILFACH DDU)

POWER STATION

LLYN PERIS

DOLBADARN CASTLE

1

2

3

LLYN PADARN

CAR PARKING

11

LLANBERIS

OLD LINE RAILWAY

TUNNEL

GLYN RHONWY QUARRY

57

60

500 M

chemical and brewing industries. In 1764, the land owner
Thomas Assherton Smith, who had inherited the Vaynol
estate, amalgamated all the independent slate workings to
form one large quarry. This was a great success, as
production was greatly increased to 3000 tons in 1793.
The quarry developed over the years with the introduction
of better transportation systems and working practices to
attain a peak of output in the late 1890's, when a work
force of some 3,000 produced 1,000,000 tons of saleable
slate. Unfortunately due to foreign imports of alternative
products and the two World Wars, the industry fell into
decline, until it finally closed in 1969. The history of the
slate industry is worthy of far more detail and we would
recommend the tour of the Slate Museum as a must.

On the final section of the walk, close to a series of
lagoons is a memorial to a tragic event which took place
on August 12th 1993. On this date a Wessex Helicopter
from RAF Valley was flying over the lake with three young
Air Cadets. This flight was a treat at the end of a course
but unfortunately the Helicopter crashed onto the lake
and the lives of the three Air Cadets were lost. The plaque
will be found close to the lake shore.

The walk L (south) along car park to pass country park
map. Along lake side and through open fields. **1.** At
metal bridge R along track. At fork go L. Into car park and
follow R.H. edge to exit. **2.** Cross road, over bridge and up
through woods to castle. Return to road, recross carpark
and return to metal bridge. Cross bridge and L along road
to pass behind Lake Railway station. **3.** R up slate steps.
4. Through wall gap to lane. L up lane and R up slate
steps. Continue up steps. **5.** At boundary fence over stile
and L along path. At lane go L. **6.** 50 metres after
building go L down path (painted sign on rock) keeping
fence on left. At Padarn country park sign L over stile and

after building go L down path (painted sign on rock) keeping fence on left. At Padarn country park sign L over stile and into Park. R and over 1/2 stile. 50 metres on, then L down through woods. **7.** At track junction R. At fork go R and on to sheet steel kissing gate. Out of park and down L. **8.** Down steep steps and cross stream by either a tree or bridge. Continue down to track. At track R uphill. **9.** At bend up to gate to join road. At road L downhill. **10.** At end of lake, L over old road bridge and L along old road. At stile at end of old road over stile and R for 60 metres then cross main road. Footpath marked Lon Las cycle way. Follow Lon Las to road. **11.** At road either walk along it or meander around lagoons. L along road to car park.

Refreshments Petes eats in Llanberis and the Heights are perennial favourites. Along in Nant Peris there is also the Vaynol Arms public house.

THE MOEL Y CI CIRCUIT

Maps 1:50,000 Sheet 115 Caernarfon and Bangor or
1:25,000 Sheet 17 Snowdon and Conwy
Distance 4.5 Miles/7 Kilometres
Height gained 800ft/242metres
Duration 2.5 Hours
Terrain Good except for the alternative which can be
muddy.
Car park In the small village of Pentir. Just off the B4409
at G.R.572670.

The car parking area is situated conveniently next to both
the Vaynol Public house and The Rainbow Court Cafe;
both these establishments being renowned for their most
excellent cuisine. This makes this particular walk
suitable for a mornings exercise as the prospect of lunch
will enhance the overall enjoyment.

Pentir is a small community little disturbed by the
passage of time. It is so peaceful that in the late 1600's
the Bishop of Bangor had a summer palace constructed
here. Indeed the power and wealth of the Bishop was
such that all the farms here abouts belonged and paid rent
to him. Through a succesion of Bishops, this land
remained in the hands of the church until the 1800's.
Later the land was purchased by the two major estates of
Penrhyn and Vaynol. In fact the boundary line between
these two estates was said to have passed through the
centre of the village of Pentir

As the walker gains height on the flanks of Moel y Ci
extensive views over the Menai Straits to the Anglesey
shore and west as far as Yr Eifl will dominate the scene.
Later as the path levels out views across to Marchlyn
Mawr and the top dam of the Dinorwig Hydro Electric

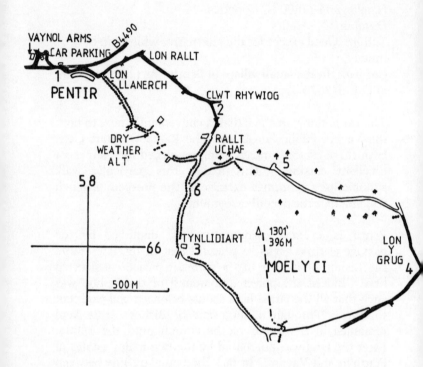

VAYNOL ARMS
CAR PARKING
B4490
LON RALLT
1
PENTIR
LON LLANERCH
CLWT RHYWIOG
2
DRY WEATHER ALT'
RALLT UCHAF
5
58
6
66
TYNLLIDIART
3
1301'
396M
MOEL Y CI
LON Y GRUG
4
500M

106

Power scheme will be seen. Behind rises the summits of Elidir Fach and Elidir Fawr. To the east views across to the higher Carneddau and the remote and majestic Cwm Llafar and the Black Ladders will be the main focus.

It is possible to visit the summit of Moel y Ci, but the going to the Trig point is over heather clad moor with no paths and as such is out of context with the rest of the walk.

The walk To commence the walk take the small road opposite the Vaynol public house. L to join and follow the main road. **1.** 50 metres after the bus shelter cross the main road to the houses opposite. Along the lane running parallel with the main road, lane later bends away continue to follow. At R bend in lane look for sign "Lôn Rallt" and up this. **2.** Continue up to second turning on R signed "Clwt Rhwyiog". Go up this lane to cottage "Rallt Uchaf". Here up grassy path which soon becomes a walled track. Continue up to cottage "Ty'n Llidiart". **3.** 1/2 L up grassy lane. When track levels and turns right go ahead through kissing gate. Go through second kissing gate (the summit can be reached from this point by turning L, at first with wall on R, then later no path or wall but a direct line uphill will reach the Trig point.) Continue along grassy path across open moorland. Through gate to road and L down it. **4.** At cross roads L along road "Lôn y Grug". At forest boundary 1/2 L up hill and along forest track. **5.** Just before track terminates, a path is seen coming in from the R, go 1/2 L along its continuation. Through kissing gate in wall corner and along grassy path, at first with wall on R. Through kissing gate and R down walled track to "Rallt Uchaf" and return to the Vaynol by the same route as you ascended.

Refreshments The Vaynol Arms and The Rainbow Court both have a well deserved reputation for their food and either can be relied upon to satisfy the hungry walker.

PORT PENRHYN, ITS RAILWAYS AND RIVERS

Maps 1:50,000 Sheet 115 Caernarfon and Bangor or
1:25,000 Sheet 17 Snowdon and Conwy.
Distance 6.5 Miles/10 Kilometres
Height gained 250ft/75 Metres
Duration 4 Hours
Terrain Very good with only a very few boggy patches.
Car park Take the turning into Port Penrhyn and turn
first L then R to park behind a small building close to the
Estate bridge. G.R 592725

The location of this walk allows one to escape the rigours
of the morning shop or even an inclement day. A low level
walk with some fine views of the northern Carneddau and
the North Wales coastal plain. The walk takes a step back
into our industrial history and the areas close association
with the slate industry. It begins in Port Penrhyn, which
was one of the principal ports of the area in the 19th
Century, exporting slate all over the world. The earliest
recorded shipment of slate was in 1570 from Aber Ogwen.
In 1730 further shipments were recorded but this time
leaving from the mouth of the Afon Cegin. It was soon
felt by the Penrhyn Estate that there was a need for a
permanent wharf, so in 1781 the estates' architect and
agent, Samuel Wyatt, was commissioned by the Pennant
family to begin a building project. This would include the
rebuilding of a medieval house (Penrhyn Castle), various
roads and also the Wharf itself. In 1786 the original lease
for the building of a wharf at the mouth of the Afon Cegin
was granted by Bishop Warren to Richard Pennant for the
sum of 20 Shillings. The development of the Port was
started in 1790 and continued with various additions
until 1855. 1852 saw the opening of the L.M.S. railway
branch line from the port to Bethesda, enabling the slate
to be shipped out by railway. 1876 saw the introduction of

steam to the narrow gauge lines. The original stone arch at the bottom of the incline into the port, through which some 1 million tons of slate per annum passed, can still be seen on the edge of the residential estate. 1880 saw the tonnage of slate being despatched by railway exceeding the tonnage being despatched by ship. In 1894, the first steam ship was introduced into the port by the Pennant family. These ships had distinctive yellow funnels topped with a black band and red dragon on either side. 1896 and 1900 saw the general strikes and lockouts at the quarry, bringing a decline to the industry. The quarries opened up again in 1903 but unfortunately with a greatly reduced output. After the 1914-18 war the occasional schooner was seen loading slate and the final shipment of slate from the port was just after the second world war. The port soon fell into decline, and currently is occupied by a number of small businesses trying to sustain a maritime tradition. The LMS railway connection was removed in 1962. None of the lines are in existence today, only the track beds. The LMS line from the port taking the higher route to join the main line by the new cricket pitch, the narrow gauge continuing to a junction close to the Bethesda line now buried under the Expressway. The bridge on the south side of the Expressway is evidence of its continuation.

The walk follows the beds of the LMS junction and the smaller gauge slate railway, which runs along the banks of the Afon Cegin. On passing under the Expressway ,the railway beds are left behind and the path crosses agricultural land to join the Afon Ogwen, following the banks of the Ogwen. Felin Willan is passed, this is still in operation for the grinding of corn. The path again passes under the Expressway to pass close to the boundary of the new rugby pitch. After crossing the old A5 road, a castellated tower comes into view, this is a vent for the railway tunnel. The path now returns to the port via the new industrial estates.

The Walk Care must be taken when driving off the main road to the car park, turn first L then R to park behind a small building close to the estate bridge. Under bridge and along bed of old railway. **1.** After second bridge path drops to a slightly lower level (split of L.M.S.). At end of Industrial Estate go on under bridge (path narrows). Carry along track and pass ford. **2.** Eventually through gate and R (along side dual carriageway). Through gate and L (under bridge for dual carriageway). L through gate. Down Bank and through gate into field (avoid turning onto rail bridge). **3.** L following field boundary. Through field gate into farm yard. Turn L and continue up to lane. L at junction continue to main road. **4.** At main road R. 75 metres cross road. Through kissing gate (timber fence on L). 15 metres, over stile R keeping fence on R. Through small gate, keeping fence on R. Over metal stile. Along grassy lane (walled). **5.** Through kissing gate to farm yard, keep wall on L. Path runs between high wall and out buildings. Up steps to cottages. L at cottages. **6.** At junction R. 9 metres the L through kissing gate. Down field keeping straight on though gate. 1/2 R cross field to R of knoll, continue to field corner. Through wall gap. Continue to final field corner. L keeping fence on L. **7.** Head under power lines towards cottages. Through kissing gates to pass in front of cottages. Cross road. Down walled path. Through kissing gate, path now runs along field boundary wall kept on R. Under power lines, through gate. Cross field walking under power lines to gate. L down field following the course of power lines. **8.** Through gate, down walled path to farm. Through farm yard and down lane. L through kissing gate. At fork R

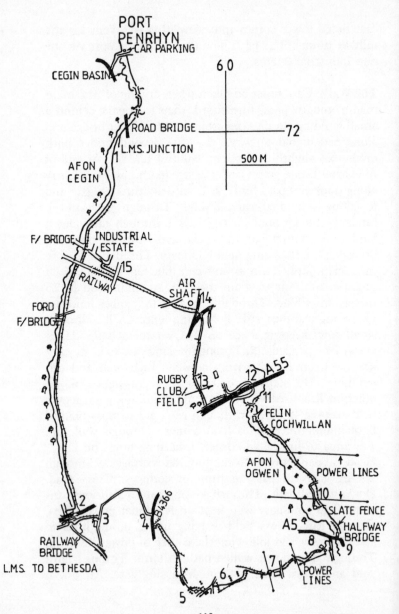

PORT
PENRHYN
CAR PARKING

CEGIN BASIN

60

ROAD BRIDGE — 72
L.M.S. JUNCTION

500 M

AFON
CEGIN

1

F/BRIDGE   INDUSTRIAL
ESTATE

15

RAILWAY

AIR
SHAFT

14

FORD

F/BRIDGE

RUGBY
CLUB/
FIELD   13   12   A55

11

FELIN
COCHWILLAN

AFON
OGWEN   POWER LINES

10

SLATE FENCE

2   B4366

A5   HALFWAY
BRIDGE

3

RAILWAY
BRIDGE   4

L.M.S. TO BETHESDA

8   9

7   POWER
LINES

5   6

down to road. L down to road junction. R over bridge to house. **9.** L down side of house. Over slate bridge. Follow slate fence, upwards, keeping fence on L. At last slate in fence head 1/2 R up field. Through field gate. Along faint track, field boundary on R. **10.** Under power lines. Through kissing gate. 2 meters L through kissing gate. Follow path down field through kissing gates, slate fence and woods on L. Down to lane passing R of water mill, Felin Cochwillan. Through gate to lane. Cross lane. Over stile. **11.** Cross field, over stile. Over footbridge. Up to service road, then down under road bridge. **12.** Up service road to bend, here go through kissing gate. Follow Rugby Club boundary wall on L. **13.**Through kissing gate, on along road. Cross service road. **14.** Cross main road. Down field keeping hedge (and railway vent tower) on R. **15.** Cross road. Down field. Over stile. L down Industrial Estate road to join railway track bed. R return to Port Penrhyn.

Refreshments There are many good establishments in or about Bangor, but the Vaynol Arms public house and the Rainbow Court in Pentir village (GR 573672) are just a short drive from the Port.

RHOSCOLYN'S COASTAL FOOTPATH

Maps 1:50,000 Sheet 114 Anglesey or 1:25,000
Rhosneigr Pathfinder sheet 750
Distance 3 Miles/5 Kilometres
Height gained 125ft/40metres
Duration 2 hours
Terrain Good hard
Car park Close to Parish church in Rhoscolyn
G.R.268757.

This coastal walk starts at the Parish church of St Gwenfaen, which dates back to the 6th century. The track soon brings the walker into open pasture lands with views across to the north coast of Holy Island with its 750 ft mountain and the South Stack lighthouse. The walk passes the memorial to the brave dog "Tyger". The stone bears the simple legend "Tyger, September 17th 1819". This commemorates the intelligence and unselfish devotion of a dog, when he saved his master, who was also Master of the ship, two crew members and a boy, from certain death. Their ketch, on passage to Liverpool in thick fog, ran aground on the Maen Piscar rock which lies 3/4 mile offshore. This rock is an isolated pinnacle in otherwise deep water and the swell soon made the ketch slip off the rock and begin to sink. The crew were forced into the water, where due to the fog they were clueless as to which way the land lay. The dogs' vociferous barking indicated that he at least knew where the land was, possibly due to his acute hearing detecting an echo from the cliffs. His master realising that their only chance of survival lay in trusting the dogs instinct, struck out for the shore, calling his crew to do the same. The master, who was a particularly good swimmer, helped the two men in turn, whilst the boy hung onto Tyger's collar. After a long struggle, the cliffs were sighted through the fog. By now they were all so exhausted that it is doubtful whether any one of them would have reached safety had it not been for the gallant efforts of the dog. Tyger, having brought the boy safely to within reach of the rocks, instead of scrambling ashore, returned to his master. His master seeing one of his crew struggling behind sent Tyger to his aid. The dog swam bravely on and grasping the man by the collar helped him to reach land. The dog carried out this act two more times, assisting his master and the other crew member to finally reach the shore. Here, they all lay in a state of complete exhaustion and Tyger, his great heart broken with the effort, feebly licked the hand of his master and died.

Close by is the Black Arch, once a site of a vast quarry which supplied marble for the Cathedrals at Bristol, Peterborough and Worcester. The path also passes the White Arch where china clay was extracted.

When passing the coast guard lookout a number of small islands can be seen offshore. These are known as "Beacon rocks" or Ynysoedd Gwylanod. The beacon after which they were named was erected to act as a warning of the rocks hereabouts. They were also used to store food for stranded mariners who may have ignored the sign, but no food is left there now.

On return to the church it is well worth visiting the graveyard to inspect the ornate memorial to Coxswain Owen Owens and four of his brave crew. They lost their lives whilst out on service on the last rescue performed by the Rhoscolyn Lifeboat, the "Ramon Cabrera". In a gallant attempt to rescue the crew members of the SS Timbo in distress on the Caernarfon bar their own vessel foundered. The graveyard also contains the graves of

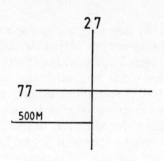

27

77

500M

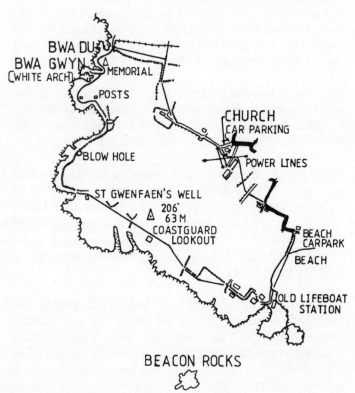

BWA DU
BWA GWYN
(WHITE ARCH)   MEMORIAL

POSTS

CHURCH
CAR PARKING

BLOW HOLE

POWER LINES

ST GWENFAEN'S WELL

206°
63M
COASTGUARD
LOOKOUT

BEACH
CARPARK

BEACH

OLD LIFEBOAT
STATION

BEACON ROCKS

many sailors from all parts of the world. They are perhaps forgotten or their final resting place is unknown to their families overseas.

The walk From the carpark up the tarred lane (Sign for the Old Rectory Guest House). When the lane becomes rough continue to the farm wall. Cross R to kissing gate. **1.** Through kissing gate and down to field boundary, keeping wall on R. Keep on across field to next kissing gate. Continue with wall on L. **2.** Through wall gap. L keeping wall on L. Over stile and 1/2 L to next stile. Continue through shallow gully to line of boulders on immediate skyline. **3.** R for 26 metres to memorial to Tyger. Follow faint path around cove, keeping close to cliff edge. **4.** Descend narrow path (over White Arch) to millstone, return to cliff top. R continuing along cliff path to pass two timber posts. **5.** Descend to wall corner nearest cliff edge following wooden steps, keeping wall on L. Continue over bridge and then stile keeping wall on L **6.** Through kissing gate at end of high wall, and then head 1/2 R towards coast guard lookout on skyline. Continue along grassy track which runs downhill towards houses. **7.** Through kissing gate and continue with wall on L. At wall corner follow faint path across field 1/2 L to stile in wall. Over stile and 1/2 L crossing lane to walled path. Follow this to garden. **8.** Cross garden keeping close to R.H. wall, to wall gap, then L down lane. Lane passes a beach on RH side. Keep on along lane descending to and along the beach, keeping sea wall on L. (On high tides a path can be followed to the left along the top of the sea wall.) Through car park and along road. **9.** At R.H. bend with tall house on corner keep on through large gate and on along walled path to R of cottage. Through kissing gate and cross field keeping wall on R. Cross lane and through kissing gate. Cross field to next kissing gate, here 1/2 L crossing field to wall corner of old orchard and stile.   **10.** Cross field to L.H. Cemetery corner, close to power lines, path runs behind Church to join lane. R down to car park.

Refreshments The White Eagle is conveniently close by and until recently was one of the few pubs which also served as the local post office. Y Gegin Fach in Four Mile Bridge is probably the closest cafe, as well as serving good food, whilst their are some seasonal cafes in Treaddur Bay.

LLYN COWLYD AND THE TAL Y BRAICH LEAT

Maps 1:50,000 Sheet 115 Caernarfon and Bangor and 1:
25,000 Sheet 17 Snowdon and Conwy
Distance 7 Miles/11Kilometres
Height gained 400ft/125metres
Duration 4 Hours
Terrain Wet and tussocky to leat then easy
Car park Situated in the village of Capel Curig behind the
shops and past the public toilet G.R. 721 581

This walk takes you into the largest stretch of open
heather moorland in the Ogwen valley with views of
Tryfan, the Carneddau and Gallt yr Ogof. When the leat
is gained the darkened waters of Llyn Cowlyd come into
view flanked by the towering shoulders of Pen Llithrig y
Wrach and Creigiau Gleision. The 260 Acre lake is the
water supply to Conwy and Colwyn Bay and the pipes for
this run underground. Those pipes running over ground
are for the Hydro Electric power station at Dolgarrog. The
first power station was built in 1908, but this was
destroyed when the Cwm Eigiau dam was breached on the
2nd of November 1925. It is said that the cause of the
failure of the dam was due to a number of circumstances.
There had been very heavy rainfall prior to the disaster
with 25 inches of rain falling in 5 days, plus a period of
high winds and the poor condition of the retaining wall
due to its hurried construction, all led to a wall
sufficiently weakened that it collapsed. During the
disaster 17 lives were lost. One old lady miraculously
survived by clinging to a piece of furniture which was
being swept along the River Conwy. Fortunately she was
brought to dry land before she was swept out to sea.

The walk returns to the main A5 road to pick up an old
road into Capel Curig. As is common in the area this road

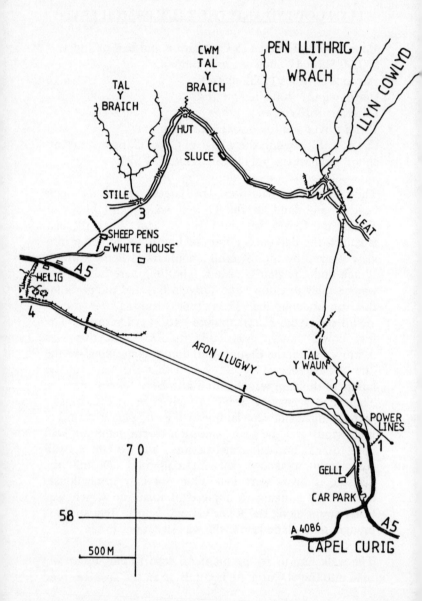

TAL Y BRAICH

CWM TAL Y BRAICH

PEN LLITHRIG Y WRACH

LLYN COWLYD

HUT

SLUCE

STILE

3

SHEEP PENS

"WHITE HOUSE"

A5

HELIG

4

2

LEAT

AFON LLUGWY

TAL Y WAUN

POWER LINES

1

GELLI

CAR PARK

A4086

A5

CAPEL CURIG

7 0

58

500M

120

is ascribed to the Romans. The truth is that the road was built by Lord Penrhyn beginning in 1797 as an extension to the road from the Hone stone quarry at Ogwen. The road went to the Capel Curig Inn, which he had constructed in 1800. Tradition has it that Lord Penrhyn had this road constructed and open to the public following his failure to be elected as an M.P. In the election the people of Conwy voted against him and he subsequently failed in his ambition. Following his defeat he swore that he would make the grass grow in the streets of Conwy. Thus he provided an alternative route for travellers, which avoided the perilous coastal section of the now A55 in the area of Penmaenmawr. He did in fact achieve his oath since much of the traffic to Chester travelled along this new route, thus depriving Conwy of its trade. He later built the spacious Royal Hotel in the hope of attracting travellers from Chester to the new packet station in Porth Dinllaen. The hotel is now Plas y Brenin (King's Palace) owned by the Sports Council for Wales and run as a mountaineering centre.

The walk Down to main road junction and turn L along A5 to walk in N direction for 500 metres. **1.** At public footpath sign leave road and follow path. Path at first runs parallel with power lines to pass right of farm. Follow wall on L to stile, over stile and R. On up to open moorland, path wet and faint in places, heading towards dip between Pen Llithrig y Wrach and Cregiau Gleision. **2.** On gaining leat it is possible to make a diversion to see the lake or turn L to follow leat. **3.** Pass a number of bridges. At bridge with opening in fence and stile on R bank follow path 1/3 L. Later down towards white house with sheep pens. Keep on with pens on L, over stile and descend to track. R to main road. Cross main road and over stile (footpath markers). Follow walled and fenced path to wooded area. **4.** Through gate and at track junction L. Along track, pass L of farm and on down to car park.

Refreshments The Pinnacle cafe in Capel Curig or The Bryn Tyrch for bar meals with a vegetarian emphasis.

Further Reading

The Best Pubs in North Wales	**Mike Dunn**
Pub Walks in North Wales	**Jim Knowles**
Bless them all	**Reg Chambers Jones**
No Landing Place	**Edward Doylerush**
Sarn Helen	**J Cantrell and A Rylance**
Death Blast in Snowdonia	**T Merion Hughes**
Great Walks in Snowdonia	**Frank Duerden**
Delving in Dinorwig	**Douglas C Carrington**
The complete guide to Snowdon	**Robert Jones**
Place names in the 3000ft Mountains of Wales	**Terry Batt**
The Lakes of Eryri	**Geraint Roberts**
Rumours and Oddities from North Wales	**Merion Evans and Wayne Evans**
Slate Quarrying in Wales	**Alun John Richards**
The Gazetteer of Slate Quarries in Wales	**Alun John Richards**
Bangor and its Port	**Ellis Williams**
Early Aviation in Wales	**Roy Sloan**
Wings of War over Gwynedd	**Roy Sloan**

MORE WALKING BOOKS FROM
GWASG CARREG GWALCH

SNOWDONIA WALKS BY DON HINSON

PEMBROKESHIRE WALKS

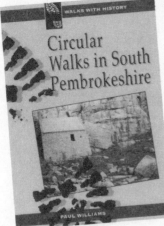

LLŶN PENINSULA WALKS

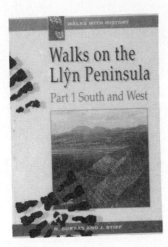